George Gissing
A Bibliography

George Gissing
A Bibliography

Michael Collie

University of Toronto Press
Toronto and Buffalo

© University of Toronto Press 1975
Toronto and Buffalo
Printed in Canada

Library of Congress Cataloging in Publication Data

Collie, Michael.
  George Gissing: A Bibliography

  Includes index.
  I. Gissing, George Robert, 1857–1903 – Bibliography. I. Title.
z8346.c65 [PR4717] 016.823'8   75–22129
ISBN 0–8020–5330–0

Contents

Acknowledgements

This book has been published with the help of grants from the Humanities Research Council of Canada, using funds provided by the Canada Council, and from the Publications Fund of the University of Toronto Press. I am also deeply indebted to the Canada Council for the original research grant which made possible many visits to American research libraries with Gissing holdings.

It is a pleasure to have this opportunity to thank members of staff at those libraries for their help and friendliness. Visits to the Beinecke Rare Book Room and Manuscript Library at Yale, the Berg Collection in the New York Public Library, the Miriam Lutcher Stark Library in the University of Texas at Austin, the Henry E. Huntington Library at San Marino, and the Pforzheimer Library in New York were invariably enjoyable and stimulating as well as useful. Without such generosity, books of this kind would be impossible.

I thank also Elizabeth Hardolf and Daphne Pan at York University for assisting me on matters of detail – a very large number of them! Miss Pan's doctoral dissertation on Gissing's revision of his own work has a direct relevance to the present book, even though our conclusions do not tally in every instance: her detailed work on Gissing's manuscripts facilitated the establishment of copy-text in a number of cases. Miss Hardolf also helped with textual collation where close comparison of printed texts proved necessary. The labours of textual scrutiny were rendered tolerable by their assistance and I am most grateful for it.

Once again I am happily beholden to my friend and colleague, Margaret Bowman, who from the outset shared the work of making this book. 'Les abeilles quittent les cavernes à la recherche des plus hauts arbres dans la lumière. Et il n'est plus question d'agir ni de compter . . .'

I thank Yale University Library for permission to quote the Memorandum of Agreement between Gissing and Remington dated 26 February 1880, in the Beinecke Rare Book Room and Manuscript Library; the Carl and Lily Pforzheimer Foundation Inc., for permission to quote and refer to autograph letters and manuscripts in the Pforzheimer Library; and the Henry W. and Albert A. Berg Collection in the New York Public Library, Astor, Lenox and Tilden Foundations, for permission to quote from George Gissing's diary and autograph correspondence now in the Berg Collection.

Abbreviations

Adams
Adams, G.M. 'How and Why I Collect George Gissing,' *Colophon, XVIII* (September 1934)

Beinecke
The Beinecke Rare Book Room and Manuscript Library, Yale University, New Haven, Connecticut

Berg
The Berg Collection of the New York Public Library

Bertz
The Letters of George Gissing to Eduard Bertz, 1887–1903, edited by A.C. Young, New Brunswick, NJ: Rutgers University Press 1961; London: Constable 1961

Diary
Gissing's diary in the Berg Collection of the New York Public Library, currently being edited for publication by Pierre Coustillas

Fleury
The Letters of George Gissing to Gabrielle Fleury, edited by Pierre Coustillas, New York Public Library 1964

GGB
'A George Gissing Bibliography' by John Spiers and Pierre Coustillas, *The Book Collecting and Library Monthly*, September, October, November 1969

Huntington
The Henry E. Huntington Library, San Marino, California

Korg
Jacob Korg, *George Gissing: A Critical Biography*, Seattle: Washington University Press 1963; London: Methuen 1965

Letters
Letters of George Gissing to Members of His Family, Collected and arranged by Algernon and Ellen Gissing, London: Constable 1927

NBL
The Rediscovery of George Gissing: A Reader's Guide, John Spiers and Pierre Coustillas, National Book League, London 1971

Notebook
Unpublished notebook in the Beinecke Library in which, amongst other things,
Gissing briefly recorded business transactions

Pforzheimer
The Carl H. and Lily Pforzheimer Library, New York City

Stark
The Miriam Lutcher Stark Library, University of Texas, Austin

Wells
Royal A. Gettman, *George Gissing and H.G. Wells*, London: Rupert Hart-
Davis 1961

Preface

At Sotheby's on 14 December 1971, eight pages of an autograph manuscript of Gissing's *Veranilda* moved from private hands to those of a dealer, evidence enough that more time must pass before anyone will be able to attempt a completely authoritative statement about Gissing's career as a novelist. In the same sale, a number of previously unknown letters was also sold. No doubt other letters, perhaps important ones, will turn up during the next decade or two.

Meanwhile, Gissing studies are in a strange state. Recent publications seem to show that there is renewed interest in his work: Gillian Tindall's *The Born Exile*, for example, is a critical book of a type that scarcely would have been possible ten years ago. The inclusion of Gissing in Routledge's Critical Heritage series is another instance of this growing interest. On the other hand, there is as yet no bibliography, no biography (except Korg's, which has a distinctly critical emphasis), no collection of the letters, no major critical work (ie, one which attempts to come to terms with all his work), and no modern editions of the novels (reissues have invariably been of the unrevised texts). This is an extraordinary state of affairs reflecting, no doubt, the prestige of the great tradition in which only 'moral' books are regarded as 'great.' This is not to say that nothing at all has been done. On the contrary, a great deal has been achieved during the last fifteen years.

There exist excellent compilations and editions to which anyone who thinks seriously about Gissing must be indebted: A.C. Young's edition of the letters of Gissing to Bertz; R.A. Gettman's book, *George Gissing and H.G. Wells;* and Pierre Coustillas' edition of Gissing's letters to Gabrielle Fleury. In addition the publications by Pierre Coustillas through the Enitharmon Press are all extremely useful additions to the stock of knowledge, especially number 3 in the series, *Henry Hick's Recollections of Gissing*, 1972, and number 7, *Letters to Edward Clodd*, 1973. (The most important secondary sources are listed in Appendix B.) Similarly, from among the many library collections of Gissing material, few would dispute the justice of mentioning in particular those in the Beinecke Library at Yale, in the Berg Collection of the New York Public Library, and in the Carl H. Pforzheimer Library. These collections contain many hundreds of letters, several notebooks, a diary (now, in 1975, being edited by Pierre Coustillas), and a number of publishers' contracts, as well as the autograph manuscripts of the majority of the novels, so that there is no dearth, obviously, of basic information about Gissing.

Yet scholarship and criticism have not proceeded hand in hand. Despite sustained research based upon the Gissing papers, critical books and articles about Gissing tend to be exclamations of discovery. For example, the National Book League's catalogue to its 1971 exhibition was entitled: 'The Rediscovery of George Gissing.' Was he lost? This emphasis upon discovery, as opposed to critical writing based upon a widely known and established foundation of fact, has a number of causes. First, the facts of Gissing's writing life, though known, have not been published. Second, spurious biographical writing on Gissing at the beginning of the century has been an obstacle to any real understanding of Gissing's purposes as a writer. Third, despite protestations to the contrary, his novels have not been generally or continuously available. Fourth, well-intentioned twentieth-century reissues have frequently been of the wrong, this is to say the unrevised, texts. Fifthly, Gissing, the man, is so fascinating that people have tended to disregard Gissing, the writer. The present work rests upon the idea that there is need, for the general reader, the student, and the book dealer, for a simple account of Gissing's publishing life.

It is within this context that the present bibliography has been prepared. No bibliography exists. No full bibliography has ever existed, though there have been several useful guides. This one is not a listing of all Gissing's titles. Rather, it is a listing of all the books published during his lifetime, together with the first appearance of works published posthumously. The main entries, as the table of contents shows, are arranged in order of first publication, while within the main entry the subsequent editions and reissues that appeared during Gissing's lifetime are also described. The bibliographical and textual relation of editions and reissues is always significant. In the case of Gissing's work, failure to relate the first edition to subsequent editions and reissues correctly has resulted in considerable confusion. For this reason, books of the one title are grouped together within the main entry, since in each case the examination of the books themselves and a collation of texts leads to a brief but definite publishing history of the book concerned. The publication history of Gissing's work as a whole is, however, more easily seen in the volume by volume chronological listing which is provided as Appendix c.

Posthumous reissues of Gissing titles that first appeared during his lifetime will be discussed briefly in the introduction. They are interesting, chiefly, because they illustrate the degeneration of the text during a sixty-year period which saw a slight rise and a vast decline in Gissing's reputation. Between 1903 and 1960 no attempt was made to edit the text of any reissue, which means that there is a particularly drab publishing period between the author's death and the renewal of interest in Gissing in the early sixties. The emphasis of the present bibliography is thus really one of priority. As a vital first step towards an authoritative description of Gissing's publishing life, the establishment of the text is essential. It is essential, for example, to establish the relation between the first and second editions of *Thyrza*, so that the reasons for regarding the second edition as the definitive text can be seen clearly. These remarks are not, of course, intended to disparage any future attempt to enumerate all Gissing reissues from 1903 to the present, but rather to state as unequivocally as possible the immediate practical purposes of the bibliography as it now stands. Incidentally, works about Gissing have recently been listed in *George Gissing: An Annotated Bibliography of Writings about Him*, compiled and edited by Joseph Wolff, Northern Illinois University Press 1973.

Two further decisions about the structure of the bibliography must be noted in the preface. The one concerns serial publications, the other the publication of limited editions from private presses. Neither has been included. An accurate listing of Gissing's short stories has been published by Pierre Coustillas in *English Literature in Transition*, 7, no. 2 (1964) 59–72. To duplicate this list seems quite unnecessary. The question of whether to include as main entries the small number of private printings was more difficult to resolve, but when in the end it was decided to classify them as only mildly interesting ephemera the chief reason was that, from the vantage point of 1975, not one of them enjoys a crucial position in the Gissing canon.

The exclusion of privately printed 'publications' from the main listing are as follows:

1 *Letters to Edward Clodd*, London 1914. Printed for T.J. Wise in an edition limited to thirty copies, in crimson paper wrappers. (A contemporary reader would refer in the first instance to *The Letters of George Gissing to Edward Clodd*, ed. Pierre Coustillas, Enitharmon Press 1974.)

2 *Letters to an Editor*, privately printed, 1915. Eleven letters from George Gissing to Clement Shorter about Gissing's contributions to *The English Illustrated Magazine*, *The Sketch*, and *The Illustrated London News*. Twenty-five copies, in olive-green paper wrappers, were printed 'for distribution among his friends.'

3 *An Heiress on Condition*, Philadelphia 1923. Forty-eight copies privately printed for the Pennell Club.

4 *Letters to Joseph Conrad*, London 1926. Twenty letters edited by G.J. Aubry and privately printed for the First Edition Club.

5 *A Yorkshire Lass*, New York 1928.

6 *Autobiographical Notes with Comments upon Tennyson and Huxley*, Edinburgh 1930. Printed 'for private circulation only' by the Dunedin Press.

Lest anyone unfamiliar with Gissing should be misled by the title of the last of these works, it must be mentioned that autobiographical information in these three letters to Edward Clodd is so slight as to be almost non-existent.

The only other volume which deserves special mention, though it is neither a first edition in the strict sense nor a limited and private printing like the six mentioned above, is *Selections Autobiographical and Imaginative from the Works of George Gissing*, with biographical and critical notes by his son and with an introduction by Virginia Woolf, published by Jonathan Cape in 1929. Historically interesting because of the insight, at an early date, into Gissing's work, this compilation is nonetheless wholly derivative and cannot be classified properly as a Gissing publication.

The relative rarity of early editions of Gissing was discussed by John Spiers and Pierre Coustillas in three articles in the *Book Collecting and Library Monthly* (September, October, and November 1969). These articles have provided a good starting point for the book collector, though a number of the books listed as rare can be found more easily in North America than in the UK. Not surprisingly, the first ten of Gissing's novels are the most rare, the revised single-volume editions of those same novels coming a close second. In particular, it seems that copies of the 6/– reprints by Smith, Elder and their cheaper reissues from the same plates, are quite difficult to come by. This fact has its implication for the present bibliography since it underscores the need, not for simple enumeration, but rather a description of the way in which books that appeared in Gissing's lifetime relate to each other. The general reader who picks up a single volume is at present without a guide.

To the end of his life, Gissing lamented the fact that as his reputation increased the sale of his books, if anything, decreased. 'The old contradiction is still in force,' he wrote to Bertz in 1902, 'my fame brings me no money, my books have only the smallest sale.' The purpose of this bibliography would have been served if the more definite identification of the books themselves led to a more profound appreciation of what Gissing wrote.

George Gissing
A Bibliography

Introduction

George Gissing was a Bohemian who was never able to visit Bohemia. He was born in exile. Between 1876 and 1903, he wrote twenty-two published and at least five unpublished novels, more than a hundred and fifty short stories, three other prose works of book length, and a certain amount of literary criticism. He paid the penalties associated with unremitting toil. The Bohemian nature was largely concealed by mere work. He worked so hard that he allowed time neither for a personal life in any true sense, nor for the normal, modest activities by which people promote their own books. One of the results of Gissing's decision to devote his life to writing, whatever else had to be denied, was that he came to be seen as a man whose domestic life was so disagreeable that it influenced everything he did and wrote. In fact, his domestic life was disagreeable because he did and wrote so much. Literature always came first. Indeed, he left two wives and the two children of his second marriage in order to remain free to write. Yet from that world of letters which he imagined as being free of restrictive social, religious, and moral standards he remained, of necessity, an exile. As Gabrielle Fleury pointed out, he was incapable of simple happiness.

Though an exile from his proper home, he travelled extensively, at least judged by the standards of the time. Having grown up in Wakefield, he lived in Manchester as a student, in Boston, Waltham, Chicago, and various places in New York state during his year in North America (1876–7), in London (1877–90 and 1895–7), in Exeter and one or two other places in the West Country (1891–5), in Siena where he wrote his book on Dickens (1897), in other parts of Italy (1898–9), in Sicily, in Greece (1889), in Paris (1899–1901), and in the Pyrenees (1902–3), as well as for short periods in other parts of France. He travelled through life incognito. Abroad, there was no need to keep up appearances. He could eat simply, live in cheap lodgings, talk freely – as an identifiable alien – with whomever he met, and be responsible to no one. Meanwhile Gissing knew London like the back of his hand and wrote books about English urban life which, as he observed himself, no one else was then in a position to write. There was no contradiction, of course, in his living away from but writing about England. His detached regard was of something he knew very well indeed.

As a type of spiritual exile, Gissing was able to make himself the least insular of the English writers of the period in which he lived. One does not doubt that early formative experiences – ones Gissing had before words like *déclassé* and Bohemian had meaning for him – were also important. For example, Gissing received from his father, who was an amateur botanist, a training in close observation and minute description. From his sister, Ellen, on whom he seems to have depended in times of stress, he gained an insight into the feminine mind which probably influenced his manner of shaping many women characters in his novels. Nevertheless, what distinguishes Gissing is his freedom intellectually – a fierce determination, which is not uncommon among people who have a solitary existence 'out of society,' to come to terms with the thoughts and issues of the day – and there can be no understanding of him, as a person, which does not take into account his emancipation from the commonplaces and influences of the time. Emancipation from commonplaces and influences, however, also meant separation from the society in which he expected to publish his novels. A person interested in Gissing's books is therefore quickly confronted with something of a paradox. On the one side, he comes to see that Gissing's development as a writer derives from a sustained preoccupation with emancipation, his own and his characters', so that quite apart from whether particular novels are successful or not they relate, most of them, to a view of the world in which the individual and the social can never be reconciled. On the other, the contemporary bibliophile soon realizes that the difficulties Gissing had with his publishers were simply a feature of a larger social alienation and that, although he was always grumbling about poor sales and so forth, he in fact never bothered to think about his own business interests, remained ignorant of publishers' practices, harboured a quaint idealistic view of the publisher's role, and was satisfied for many years to sell the copyright outright because he knew he could live on that amount of money, however small, until he had written his next book. Consequently, one knows quite a lot about Gissing's development as a man of letters, very little about his business affairs. Beyond the occasional opinion on the colour of a binding, Gissing had no interest in the physical manufacture of his books and scarcely any interest in sales apart from a vague, romantic idea of literary reputation. It is partly because he lacked any kind of business sense that he provides such a good example of late nineteenth-century publishing practice. His publishers did as they wished. Meanwhile Gissing did as he wished. His difficulties with publishers confirmed his notion that he was not pandering to the public! His freedom to write as he wished, even badly, remained important to him throughout his life and one can say, therefore, that he took the novel form and used it for his own purposes, provided one knows what kind of person he was and what were his purposes. He was not a man dogged by circumstance and domestic misery but, as it were, a potential contributor to the *Fortnightly Review* who preferred to write novels. Of this free intellectual life a few salient features may be mentioned at the outset.

First, he read Robert Owen, Bentham, J.S. Mill, Comte, became a Positivist, met Frederic Harrison, attended 'positivist' gatherings, associated himself with popular socialist movements, attended meetings and rallies, made a few speeches himself, watched the career of people like William Morris with a keen eye, found the optimism of the socialist unacceptable and, finally, having lived through it all, opted out of the world of popular movements and abandoned the idea of progress and purposeful social development. He was as well aware as anyone, in other words, not merely of the social conditions of contemporary urban England but also of the way in which people had thought about them. All this before 1885. Second, he had throughout his writing life a scholar's understanding of Greek and Latin literature. He made his living by teaching Latin in his early years and the diaries show that he retained his facility with the language and his love of the literature to the end of his life. Third, he was a good linguist. He read, wrote, and spoke French with ease. He had a good command of German and Italian. At the end of his life he learnt Spanish. In a lifetime devoted to books of all kinds, he read Turgenev, Ibsen, Dostoievski, George Sand, Daudet, and Zola, in German and French, well before their works were widely known in England. He was one of the first modern Englishmen to be a genuine European man of letters. Fourth, he was an insatiable reader, never happy when away from a large library, marking in his diary days or periods when he did *not* read, and, until he became ill, tireless in his attempts to come to terms with a masterpiece as, for example, when he first read Dante. These are some of the ways in which his independence of mind manifested itself, though it is more difficult to trace to its source his determination to be free and independent, both as a person and as a writer. Contrary to the general view of him, incidentally, there were many things which gave him genuine, albeit private pleasure: his books; sculling on the Thames; ancient history; visiting and brooding over places mentioned by classical writers; hard work; the work of contemporary writers such as Meredith. An intelligent, knowledgeable, and well-informed person, he was simply incapable of the compromises and accommodations by which most people manage their day by day existence. *He* knew he was a contemporary European man of letters. Others did not. Indeed many of his immediate friends would not even have understood the concept. From their point of view, he was a rebel, a perverse nonconformist, a failure.

Most writers are to a certain extent egotistical. They have to be. Gissing was completely egotistical. How else could he have put everything else aside in order to write and publish a book a year through his working life? The single-mindedness with which he pursued his main course is both impressive and rather frightening. The body of work he produced by the age of forty-six is impressive; the sacrifices he was prepared to make for the sake of his work frightening. He sacrified both his private and his public, professional life, both his wives and his publishers, so much so that he seemed insensitive to other people and uncompromising in his rejection of them, and at the same time foolish in that he denied himself the help that other writers have had and that he needed. On the other hand, he was probably more sinned against than sinning. It is not unreasonable for a man to expect fair treatment from a wife or a publisher. If things go badly in one part of his life, there will be compensations in the other. Gissing was badly treated by two wives and two publishers. In a short life, he had more than his fair share of ill fortune, the serious and long illness which led to his death robbing him of the chance to enjoy even the slow growth of his reputation as a writer. He experienced few of the pleasures of uninhibited friendship and never saw one of his books received with complete enthusiasm. When he died abroad in 1903, few people were aware of the extent and nature of his work or of the difficulties he had had to overcome.

The wives and the publishers: how do they fit into a life so devoted to literature that everything else was regarded as of secondary importance?

It is scarcely surprising that Gissing, the man, and Gissing, the writer, were in conflict. Gissing, the man, wanted or thought he wanted the normal pleasures and satisfactions of life. Gissing, the writer, wanted freedom to read and write without intrusion of any kind. If he had to set himself a tough routine, as for example during the period in which he tutored private pupils from 7 AM to 5 PM each day and between 6 PM and midnight wrote – a routine which he maintained, remorselessly, until the novel was finished, he expected others to accept the fact that, unless it were done in this way, it would not be done at all. Like many others before and since he wanted two lives. Nor is it surprising that he wrote his best work when he was by himself, but that when he was by himself he was miserable and longed for companionship, as perhaps this brief review of his career will, amongst other things, show.

Gissing spent the first part of his career as a novelist with Helen Harrison, whom he probably met in Manchester in 1875. When he returned to England in 1877 from the United States he went almost immediately to London and Helen Harrison either went with him or followed him. In 1879 they were married and lived in various rooms and sets of rooms in various parts of London, Gissing then and later having difficulty in finding lodgings in which he could write undisturbed. Slowly, very slowly, he began to earn enough from tutoring to exist, but during these early years they were very poor, living as they did entirely by themselves. His first complete novel was rejected and at least five publishers had rejected his second, *Workers in the Dawn*, before, in 1880 when Gissing was 22, he published it at his own expense with Remington. His next work, *Mrs. Grundy's Enemies*, was started almost immediately, was accepted by Bentley who paid Gissing £50 for it, but was never published. How Helen Harrison spent her life during this period is not known. Next to nothing is known about her. It is difficult to believe that a relationship that had survived Gissing's expulsion from Owens College, a long separation and a reunion, the probability that they lived with each other before they were married, and then their marriage, depended solely – as has so often been suggested – on Gissing's desire to 'reform' someone of 'low' character. Pious talk. It is more probable, as well as more humane, to suppose that at least between 1876 and 1880 Gissing and Helen Harrison liked being together.

On the other hand, the strain of living with someone who worked unremittingly, and liked it, must have been considerable. It is said on the evidence of Morley Roberts that Helen was a prostitute and on the evidence of the early novels, particularly *The Unclassed*, that she always had been, or in London became, an alcoholic. Flimsy evidence indeed. That she became ill is certain, though whether the illness was the cause or the result of the breakdown of the marriage has not been determined. Here again one awaits a proper biography. At all events, in 1882 Gissing arranged for her to go to a 'home' in Battersea and though she left it at least twice to return to him, he refused to live with her again. Matrimonial agreements or disagreements tend to defy analysis and for as long as one knows only one side of the matter, Gissing's, a fair understanding of what happened is probably impossible. Maybe she drank, refused to leave, let him down, and embarrassed him. Maybe he refused her the companionship she had every reason to expect. Maybe neither of them really knew what was happening. Gissing tended to attribute to social causes things that others regard as matters of personal responsibility. Thus, though he was quite capable of decisive action, he never regarded himself as responsible for anything that happened to him. When he heard of Helen's death in 1888 and went to see her, he at first could not recognize her. 'I looked long, long at her face, but could not recognize it. It is more than three years, I think, since I saw her, & she has changed horribly. Came home to a bad wretched night. In nothing am I to blame; I did my utmost; again & again I had her back with me. Fate was too strong. But as I stood beside that bed, I felt that my life henceforth had a firmer purpose. Henceforth I never cease to bear testimony against the accursed social order that brings about things of this kind' (*Diary*). Fate often figures prominently in rationalizations about the disintegration of marriages. As perhaps it must.

Whatever the rights and wrongs of the matter, Gissing lived by himself, at first in lodgings and then in a flat near Baker Street Station, between 1882 and 1891. During this period he wrote and published the uneven but strong early work on which his reputation must chiefly depend: *The Unclassed* (1884),

Isabel Clarendon (1886), *Demos* (1886), *Thyrza* (1887), *A Life's Morning* (1888), *The Nether World* (1889), and *The Emancipated* (1890). Of these novels, *The Unclassed* and *Isabel Clarendon* were in different ways apprentice work, though the former marks a particularly interesting stage in his development. The novels which immediately followed, however, showed a marked increase in his powers. He attempted to create fictions within a grim, contemporary urban context that did not have undue recourse to Romantic convention, that did not exclude as 'unliterary' the urgent social and political questions of the day, that captured the unheroic lives of ordinary people whose thoughts were conditioned if not determined by the brute struggle for existence, and that involved sharp, sometimes bitter critiques of both socialist and bourgeois dreams. His novels became progressively more psychological in interest but the psychological interest was always within the context of a fundamentally pessimistic world view; ordinary people strive for ordinary honesties though at the mercy of forces that apparently cannot be controlled. What is remarkable is the range of character inhabiting this grey world: indeed one of the means by which he held the reader at a distance and precluded facile sympathy with hero or heroine was precisely this stress on an urban mosaic recreated within the confined, naturalist world of limited possibilities. It could be argued that Gissing failed to find completely satisfactory answers to the artistic problems he set himself during these years, since his lack of sympathy with the world he created gave the novels a raw, unresolved quality that alienated the reader in a different sense. It was nonetheless his best period of work.

As far as his writing was concerned, this period was terminated by the two books that have so much in common: *New Grub Street* (1891), which he wrote just before his second marriage, and *Born in Exile* (1892), which he concluded immediately after it. They are both novels which are more satisfactorily worked out than the others, chiefly because they were made to depend on situations which were not susceptible to easy resolution and which therefore did not frustrate the reader by their inconclusiveness. Or, to put this same point in a different way, Gissing now wrote about authors and intellectuals who, in a more or less credible fashion, absorbed within the range of their talk and actions whatever might have appeared in the earlier novels as a rather crude kind of authorial intrusion. He had found his own subject, though he did not think so himself.

Despite the hardship, it had been a fruitful period of his life. He was able to give up the tutoring: from 1886 he lived by his pen alone. He visited Paris in 1886. In London, he rented a flat where he remained until the end of 1890; Algernon, his brother, spent the best part of a year there and they went to plays and concerts together. He became a trifle dependent on his housekeeper,

Mrs King. And, much more important, he spent two winters abroad. In 1888-9, from October to March, he travelled in France and Italy. In 1889-90 he went to Italy and Greece. 'My life is richer a thousand times – aye, a million times, – than six months ago,' he told his sister during the first of these expeditions (*Pforzheimer*). He lived by himself, wrote, travelled, read widely, corresponded with Bertz, but was desperately lonely. The man and the writer, not surprisingly, remained in conflict.

The first mention of Gissing's having met Edith Underwood, who was to become his second wife, is the *Diary* entry for 24 September 1890. The autumn was a happy one. On Sundays they went on excursions together to places like Kew and Richmond. Edith came to Gissing's flat in the evenings. Gissing's depression lifted and during the months in which they got to know each other he quickly wrote *New Grub Street*. Then, at the end of 1890, he allowed the lease of his flat to expire and moved to Exeter.

The years that Gissing spent with Edith Underwood were quite different from either the period that preceded them or the period which followed. They were married on 25 February 1891, after Gissing had insisted that they would marry on that day – three years after Helen's death – or not at all, and lived with each other until September 1897, at first in Exeter and later back in London. Despite the fact that Gissing went to considerable lengths to ensure the solitude and freedom he needed in order to write, going to the extreme for example of renting an attic in another part of London in which he could work, his affection for Edith was not proof against the age-old trials of domestic life. They were poor. They were separated from each other by the two children. Like many other Victorian fathers, Gissing appears to have had little notion of how to cope. He records the fact, for example, that not until his son Walter was five years old did they, he and Walter, go out together without Edith. Then they spent the afternoon in the National Gallery. It is claimed, on the evidence partly of the *Diary*, partly of Gissing's letters to Algernon, that Edith was uneducated, unsuitable, vixenish, given to uproar and rowing, and incapable of managing a household in which Gissing could work. Perhaps this is true, though there is very little external evidence to corroborate it. Just as likely is the possibility that Gissing found domestic life intolerable after the freedom he had enjoyed during the previous few years. The love of a person and a hatred for domesticity are not incompatible, but the two have to be held in a nice equilibrium if nothing is to be broken.

Later on, when Gabrielle Fleury was separated from Gissing during the months he spent in a sanatorium in Suffolk, she wrote an interesting, if rather hysterical letter to Mrs H.G. Wells. Of Gissing's impatience with the way things were managed in Mme Fleury's flat in Paris where they had spent the preceding winter, she said: 'I in vain explain to him again and again the management; he does not believe me, *will* not. He is too glad to have found out a shadow to embody his latent – always latent – complaints, disquietude, discontent. You may be sure that as long as he has not found any, he dreadfully suffers from want of giving an appearance of consistency to that tormenting unquietness of soul. He *can't* be unreservedly happy; it is not in his nature; and that is what makes it really hard to sacrifice without good reason someone to him: because you know it will be a useless sacrifice.' And a little later in the same letter: ' ... sums of money required from him by Wakefield or even that woman [as they called Edith], always seem to him small and trivial indeed, but the expenses made in our household always seem extravagant, however modest and carefully managed' (*Wells* 185).

If Gabrielle Fleury could give in 1901 the candid account of Gissing's domestic attitudes that she does give in this letter to Mrs Wells, one wonders whether Edith might not have said rather the same, with as much justification, in 1895 or 1896. The marriage became more and more turbulent. Gissing spent more time away from home, and by 1896 at the latest he had become seriously ill. On doctor's orders he spent the spring and early summer of 1897 in Budleigh Salterton in Devon. After a brief period of work in which he wrote *The Town Traveller*, the family went north on a long summer holiday. It was at the end of this holiday that he sent his son, Walter, to Wakefield and then left Edith and Alfred to go to Siena. The family was never reunited.

Gissing did very little strong work during the years he spent with Edith Underwood. A great deal of his energy was dissipated in the writing of short stories, very few of which are memorable or as interesting as his novels. He wrote seven novels during the period: *Denzil Quarrier* (1892), *The Odd Women* (1893), *In the Year of Jubilee* (1894), *Eve's Ransom* (1895), *The Paying Guest* (1895), *Sleeping Fires* (1895), and *The Whirlpool* (1897), but several of them, particularly those published in 1895, were little better than pot-boilers. *New Grub Street* and *Born in Exile* had in a real sense been a turning point. Before them his novels, whatever psychological interest they may have had, depended upon the harsh gaze with which Gissing looked at contemporary urban life and his ability to recreate what he saw on the page without the intrusion of sentiment. After them he drifted away from his urban subjects without developing a technique or an art that would allow his novels to be genuinely psychological. This is not to disparage entirely the novels of the period: both *In the Year of Jubilee* and *The Whirlpool* are of considerable interest. But in the main the period is one of frustration, both personal and artistic. A biographer will show us, perhaps, at what stage his work began to be affected by his poor health. One suspects it may have been even earlier than 1895.

When Gissing left England and abandoned his family (though for the rest of his life he made Edith a weekly allowance through a solicitor and took responsibility, with help from others, for the education of his sons), he went first to Siena where, in peace at last, he wrote *Charles Dickens: A Critical Study*. Then in the first part of 1898 he travelled in Italy and Sicily, returning to England only in the third week of April. Feeling himself once more the master of his own life, he recovered some of his old energy and enthusiasm. He continued to do his best work when he was by himself. He continued to be vulnerable to acute fits of depression and loneliness when he was by himself but not working hard. The final period of his life is not an exception. Work he did, but usually in solitary confinement.

In May 1898, he settled by himself in Dorking, doing his best to conceal his whereabouts from Edith. In June, probably on 23 June, he heard from one Gabrielle Fleury who requested permission to translate *New Grub Street* into French. From the first he felt a strong attachment for her, just as he had, spontaneously, for Edith Underwood and Helen Harrison. They met in July. By October, when Gabrielle Fleury spent a week in Dorking, they had already decided to live with each other when it could be arranged. On 15 October 1898 he notes in his *Diary:* 'our life together will begin in the spring.' And it did. During the winter of 1898–9, by himself in Dorking, he wrote the first three Dickens prefaces and *The Crown of Life*, then on 7 May 1899 joined Gabrielle and her mother in Rouen, and for the next two years lived with them, mostly in their Paris flat, while he wrote the rest of the Dickens prefaces, *By the Ionian Sea*, and *Our Friend the Charlatan*.

Critics who have written about Gissing from a biographical point of view have tended to be impressed by Gissing's account, as it is taken to be, of miserable days with Edith and, largely because his effusive letters to Gabrielle have survived while such letters as he may have written to Helen and Edith have not, have assumed that his final years had a quality denied him in the years of his 'foolish' marriages, since at last he had the companionship of an educated woman of sensibility that he had referred to so longingly on many occasions throughout his life. In Gissing's correspondence with Wells, in the letter to Mrs Wells from Gabrielle Fleury which has already been quoted, in Gissing's rather sudden return to England in 1901, and in the storm in a teacup that blew up over Mme Fleury's cooking and Gissing's refusal to travel back to Paris by the direct route after his period in a sanatorium in Suffolk, one senses that he had not been tamed or domesticated. Not much more than an impression can be formed, however, since very little of a detailed kind is in fact known about those first two years with Gabrielle Fleury. What they did, how they spent their time, whom they met, what crises they survived – in other words, most of the normal details of everyday life – await the biographer. Gissing evidently corresponded with his wife during this period, though none of the letters has survived. He called Gabrielle his wife as well – an assertion that, had Gissing lived, might have proved more trouble than it was worth.

Gissing's last days were spent in the south of France. He was very weak from emphysema and other ailments, could scarcely walk, worked in short spells on a *chaise longue*, had immense difficulty breathing because of the condition of his lungs, and was in fact dying. In this awful state he managed to finish his work on Dickens, and to write *The Private Papers of Henry Ryecroft*, *Will Warburton*, and almost the whole of *Veranilda*. Despite the tension that had arisen because of Gabrielle's inability to satisfy both Gissing and her mother – Gissing had to be in a dry, warm climate, Mme Fleury could not or would not leave Paris – he did at least have Gabrielle with him during his final months, so that his last days were happy ones. Happy in a sense. *Ryecroft* of course chronicles some of the ambivalent thoughts and sensations of the European novelist who yet yearns for hearth and home in his native land. If he had not been ill, he would have had to come to terms with his sons as they grew to maturity. And if he had not been ill, Gabrielle would have had to declare herself for him, perhaps – if she had gone to him rather than he to her – with greater difficulty to herself. But this is speculation. His life was cut short and at an age when some of his contemporaries had still to do their best work.

Such is the outline of his life. He may have fared rather badly in the hands of his wives. They certainly fared badly in his. On the vexed question of the extent to which his own domestic experiences informed his work, a good case could probably be made for the argument that the gloomy atmosphere generated by his early work had a worse effect on his marriages than his marriages had on his work. From a literary point of view, one objects to the heavy biographical approach to Gissing's work, with its dreary insistence upon what he suffered because of his alleged mistakes, not so much because it is based upon quite dubious evidence, as in this introduction there has been an attempt to suggest, but more because the preoccupation with those superficialities of life that are revealed in the letters and in the *Diary* has tended to militate any other kind of critical writing about the novels themselves.

In any case, Gissing fared much worse in his dealings with publishers than in his dealings with women. Just as he failed in his relationships with people, at least until late in life, to discover a comfortable middle ground between total possession and not knowing a person at all, so in his direct dealings with publishers he failed to acquire the confidence and knowledge, the social ease and *savoir faire* that would have obliged them to deal fairly and squarely with him. He was exploited. At the time Gissing began to write in the early eighties,

Victorian publishers, and particularly the established houses, had a tendency to take advantage of their authors. Gissing, in this situation and feeling himself forever at a disadvantage, allowed himself to be exploited. As the years passed he came to be on quite good personal terms with Payn, reader for Smith, Elder, with Smith himself, and with A.H. Bullen, one of the partners in the firm of Lawrence & Bullen. Yet despite this, he had a rather subservient attitude to his early publishers, partly of necessity, partly because of an exaggerated sense of the importance of the business of letters. He was also foolish, since his perpetual need for ready cash inclined him to accept offers other men might have seen could with advantage have been refused.

The story of Gissing's dealings with his publishers, which like his biography or as part of it deserves to be told in full, provides an interesting picture of the conditions which prevailed at the end of the century. A summary is given here which will complement, it is hoped, the details which are given in the body of the text and provide at least a chronological context to which the latter n otes on individual books can be related.

Not much need be said about Remington, with whom Gissing pu blished *Workers in the Dawn* at his own expense. Though he received less than a pound in return, it was a good investment from Gissing's point of view, not co mmercially, since it did not help him to place his later work, but psychologically, since it allowed him to feel it was right to go on writing. Nor is there much point in dwelling on the initial meanness of Chapman & Hall, who published *The Unclassed* and *Isabel Clarendon*, giving him nothing at all for one and £30 for the other. Gissing merely suffered as other authors had suffered (consider Meredith, for example), though his case was an extreme one, about which Chapman & Hall appear to have felt no compunction whatever. No: it was the treatment Gissing received from Smith, Elder and from Lawrence & Bullen that deserves brief attention since their exploitation of him was so blatant and since they were the dominant influences which shaped the publishing events with which this bibliography is concerned.

With Smith, Elder Gissing published five novels: *Demos*, *Thyrza*, *A Life's Morning*, *The Nether World*, and *New Grub Street*. Except in the case of *Thyrza* he sold the copyright outright. A long account might be written of the business relationship between author and publisher, but for the purposes of this introduction two examples will suffice. The one concerns *Thyrza*; the other *New Grub Street*.

First *Thyrza*. Smith, Elder's practice at the time in question was to purchase a copyright for a flat fee and then saturate the market with versions of the book in different formats and at different prices, reprinting one or another version as public demand required. At least as far as Gissing's work was concerned, they first published the novel in three volumes, to a large extent in the hope of success with the circulating libraries. Either immediately, or as the reception of the book warranted, they then made a single-volume edition which was well bound, was printed on good paper, and was sold at 6/-. From these plates, they printed three other versions: a fairly well bound hardback on cheap paper and with an imposition which reduced the margins, to be sold at 3/6; a 'softback' bound in cheap red cloth sold at 2/6; and a paperback or 'yellowback' which was sold at 2/-. (Since this is the pattern with all five of Gissing's novels, incidentally, only example descriptions of the reissues are given in the body of the text.) *Demos*, the first novel taken by Smith, Elder, did well and was quickly reissued. There was evidently a market of some kind. Gissing noticed the reissues, some of them, as they appeared, and must have written to Smith, Elder for details, since on 6 August 1890 comes the *Diary* entry: 'Reply from Smith, Elder, saying they have sold only 412 copies of *Thyrza*, & offering £10 for copyright.' £10 is a small sum for the copyright of a book one way or the other, but one wonders whether they would have been willing to pay it if they had not expected a reasonable return from Gissing's books. Though he was about to remarry, and needed cash in hand, Gissing was foolish to accept the offer, which the *Diary* shows he did on 7 January 1891. (He did, however, revise it for them!) In point of fact, Smith, Elder not only continued to reissue Gissing's work until after his death when the business changed hands, but also on several occasions during the last ten years of his life refused to relinquish the copyright for the sake of a collected edition. They must have done fairly well from him. He did badly.

In the second of the two *Diary* entries mentioned above, Gissing noted Smith, Elder's acceptance of *New Grub Street*: 'In the evening came Edith, &, by the 8.30 post [PM or AM?] at last a letter from Smith, Elder. They think *New Grub Street* clever and original, but fear it is too gloomy. Offer £150. I wrote at once accepting, (ahem!) & asking them to add the £10 they offered for *Thyrza*. Heaven be thankit!' Smith, Elder's justification of the low offer would have been more convincing if it had not been the fifth book they had accepted. Whether they were simply making a hard, business-like offer for a good book or more cynically depending upon their knowledge that Gissing both wanted cash in hand and believed that he had a reputation for an unacceptable type of social realism does not very much matter. They had the best of the bargain. While, on the one hand, Gissing had often suffered for having written things unsuitable for Mudie's readers, most notably in Bentley's rejection of *Mrs. Grundy's Enemies* and in Payn's request that the ending of *A Life's Morning* should be altered, on the other hand, Smith, Elder were in a better position than Gissing to appreciate, first, that the moral climate had very much altered since

Gissing had had difficulty publishing his first book a dozen years earlier and, second, that there was nothing in *New Grub Street* that was so very offensive in any case. Where the firm surely went too far, and on a business level perhaps simply made a mistake, was in giving the poor sales of *New Grub Street* as a reason for not offering Gissing more than £150 for his next book, *Born in Exile* (*Diary* 7 August 1891). In fact, *New Grub Street* did well. Though the accounts are lost, other signs, particularly the reviews and the immediate reissues, indicate that the initial sales must have been quite reasonable. Had Smith, Elder chosen to act more generously, or had Gissing from a business point of view been less foolish and inexperienced, he might have been spared many of the anxieties he suffered during the period of his second marriage and indeed might have done better work. Unfortunately for him, he was entirely without common sense or business acumen.

His change of publisher from Smith, Elder to Lawrence & Bullen is noted in an interesting letter he wrote to Frederic Harrison on 29 December 1891. 'With me, little is changed; I work day after day as of old. The new publishers, Lawrence & Bullen, are bringing out my next book, a 1 vol. novel; a longer story is in the hands of A & C Black, who, however, will not publish it until towards the end of '92. The small book – *Denzil Quarrier* by name – is to appear simultaneously in England, America, Australia & on the Continent; but there is not much chance of great results. My last – *New Grub Street* – made something of a stir, & is now in a 6/- volume, I am glad to say. But it is doubtful if I shall have any more dealings with Smith & Elder; they are too narrow in their views' (*Pforzheimer*). Though Gissing was to meet A.H. Bullen in Exeter, have dinner with him, and be impressed by his interest in the classics, it would seem that the move had come from Lawrence & Bullen for, on 26 September 1891, he wrote in his *Diary*: 'Letter from Lawrence & Bullen, the new publishers, saying that Roberts has told them I am engaged on a 1 vol. story, and offering to publish it for me at 6/- giving me 1/- on each copy; also willing to pay £100 on account.' The era of the three-decker novel and of the dominance of the circulating library was ending – ending rapidly. On these terms, or terms very like them, Lawrence & Bullen were to publish six of Gissing's works: *Denzil Quarrier*, *The Odd Women*, *In the Year of Jubilee*, *Eve's Ransom*, *The Whirlpool*, and *Human Odds and Ends*, which was the only collection of short stories to be published during his lifetime. Gissing considered Lawrence & Bullen, particularly Bullen, civilized people with whom to have dealings. He retained his confidence in them to the end. Indeed he retained his confidence in them even longer than that, for no one at first bothered to tell him when the partnership had been dissolved and that the firm, as a partnership, had gone out of business.

Whether the confidence was justified is open to doubt. No doubt they wanted at the outset to have an established author on their list, which was not otherwise particularly strong. For this reason they were anxious to issue reprints or new editions of any of Gissing's earlier work, if the copyright was in hand or could be purchased, and it was in fact with their encouragement that Gissing revised and shortened four of his novels for republication as single volumes (*Workers in the Dawn*, *The Unclassed*, *Isabel Clarendon*, and *The Emancipated*, though only the second and the fourth were in fact published by them). No doubt, too, they gave him confidence to go on writing when his fortunes were at a low ebb and when he had become disillusioned with Smith, Elder. Yet what Gissing really liked about Lawrence & Bullen was, naïvely, that they gave him an advance against royalties, even though experience was to show not only that advance and royalties combined scarcely equalled the outright payments he had received from Smith, Elder, but that, judging by the size of the initial printings, they did not expect them to. Bullen sent Gissing itemized accounts but not very much money. When Colles, the agent, remonstrated about this, Gissing at first said that 'it would be too bad to go elsewhere with it after their standing by me through the evil days' (*Pforzheimer* 17 January 1895), and, more roundly, in his *Diary:* '4 pp. letter to Colles, assuring him, as he desires to know it, that L & B do not swindle me,' but then later, when tackled by his next agent, Pinker, on the same subject, acknowledged that he was only receiving about £10 a year from Lawrence & Bullen and that he would transfer away from them if there was a 'demonstrable advantage.' That was on 10 November 1899, by which time he had already 'transferred' away from them, though because of a sentimental sense of loyalty he could not bring himself to acknowledge the fact. All in all, Gissing did no better with Lawrence & Bullen than he had done with Smith, Elder. He never expected to earn very much and therefore counted himself fortunate that he had found a publisher willing to share his low fortunes in a frank and civilized manner. It would appear that when A.H. Bullen reissued the novels in 1901 on his own initiative, the partnership having by that time been dissolved, he did not bother to inform Gissing.

The third stage in Gissing's publishing life was managed by two agents, at first Colles, and then, after September 1897, Pinker. Gissing needed the help of an agent as soon as he began to spend long periods abroad and, though Gissing to some extent resented their large fees and was unwilling to return for direct discussion with publishers himself, he did with their help receive more money for some of his books, particularly as the result of the sale of foreign rights. (It is possible, incidentally, that this last detail had a bearing upon Gissing's initial reception in North America, since his early work was not issued in the United

States until after his death.) Between them Colles and Pinker placed and managed what one might call the free-lance writing of the latter part of Gissing's life: *The Paying Guest* (Cassell), *Sleeping Fires* (Unwin, *Charles Dickens* (Blackie), *The Town Traveller* and *The Crown of Life* (Methuen), and *The Private Papers of Henry Ryecroft*, *Will Warburton*, and *Veranilda* (Constable). With these agents, Gissing was at the same disadvantage – a disadvantage partly of his own making – as he had been with the earlier publishers. On 17 October 1903, for example, he wrote to Pinker about *The Private Papers of Henry Ryecroft*, which had been enjoying considerable popular success: 'I confess I had expected a rather larger yield than this (£75.6) & I must be able to settle my mind on the point, both for present and future. Also, what royalty do Dutton's pay? .. On 22nd April you reported a sale of more than 2500 in England, and more than 800 in the Colonies, & the sale has certainly gone on since' (*Pforzheimer*). Unfortunately the realization that by rating himself at too low a point he had allowed others to do likewise came too late. (See, for example, his letters to Bertz dated 26 October and 16 November 1902.) He died poor and with his affairs in disarray, after incessant labour.

Perhaps it would be going too far to suggest that his two agents had exploited him as coolly as his two principal publishers, but the publishers and agents between them were certainly as heartless in their dealings with him as any of his wives. It has sometimes been suggested that *New Grub Street* provided a good portrait both of Gissing's own difficulties as a writer and more generally of the conditions that prevailed at the time. What it in fact revealed, of course, if it revealed anything personal, was Gissing's complete ignorance of Victorian publishing.

A word must be said, finally, about the fortunes of Gissing's work since his death – or rather about the misfortunes.

The chief misfortune is that they have gone out of print. For about twenty-five years after his death 'entrepreneurial' reissues appeared from time to time, some of them from good publishing houses such as Routledge & Kegan Paul, Nelson, John Murray, and Sidgwick & Jackson. But none of these is of the slightest textual or critical significance. As far as can be ascertained, there is no evidence, between 1903 and 1963, of any edition for which either editor or publisher attempted to establish a definitive text and they are therefore not described in this bibliography, in which there is an emphasis upon first editions and on what Gissing himself wrote or rewrote. In any case, the posthumous reissues are themselves out of print and almost as scarce as the single-volume novels published during Gissing's lifetime. It must be mentioned, too, that quite apart from their prohibitive cost, the photographic reprints produced in England and in North America by the Harvester Press and by AMS respectively do not fill the need for properly edited editions of Gissing's work, since even when the correct text has been reproduced the errors of the original are retained and the correct text has *not* always been chosen. At the time of writing, of Gissing's twenty-five novels and book-length prose works, only four – *New Grub Street, Born in Exile, The Odd Women*, and *The Private Papers of Henry Ryecroft* – are available for purchase in ordinary editions. Only in the last of the four has there been an attempt to establish a definitive text. Evidently, the type of problem that has been referred to briefly in this introduction will continue to obstruct both students and ordinary readers until at least the better of Gissing's novels can be obtained and discussed more freely. What is needed is a new, properly edited, and not too expensive, edition. Until it is available, Gissing will continue to be at the mercy of people more interested in his wives than in his work.

Technical Note

Gissing was published commercially but his books did not sell. During the first part of his career, and leaving aside his first novel, his work was published by Chapman & Hall, Bentley, Smith, Elder, and Lawrence & Bullen, all of them principal London publishers. In later years, when he spent more time abroad, he had the services of literary agents who were also successful in placing his work with good publishers. On the other hand, he was not particularly successful. Whenever a novel sold reasonably well, he had usually sold the copyright. When he retained the copyright, the novel was usually no more than a modest success. Gissing never suspected the publisher of being anxious to buy the copyright of novels judged likely to be successful. The result, anyway, was that Gissing exerted no influence whatsoever on the physical form of any edition. He left everything to the publisher and refrained from asking the most elementary questions. He rarely knew how many copies had been printed. Reissues took him by surprise. His sense of the relation between novelist and publisher is seen, for example, in his willingness to revise a novel in which, because he had sold the copyright, he had no commercial interest. Consequently his books taken together represent in a very straightforward way normal contemporary publishing practice. As will be seen, this is particularly true of the books published by Smith, Elder, though more generally the pattern of new editions and reissues, representing the publisher's sense of demand and his estimate therefore of the relative success of the author, is a normal trade pattern, the only deviation of any significance being that created by *By the Ionian Sea*. The relatively simple procedures adopted in this bibliography are seen as being compatible with this simple publishing pattern.

Throughout the bibliography the words 'edition' and 'issue' or 'reissue' are used in an orthodox way. It has not proved necessary to distinguish between single copies of particular editions or issues. The instances where there is disturbance of any kind *within* an edition or issue are recorded, but there are only a few such instances. This is stressed because the task of checking subsequent editions and reissues during Gissing's lifetime proved to be particularly exacting, especially in the case of the novels published by Smith, Elder. A very large number of single copies have been examined and one therefore asserts with confidence (though, alas, not with *final* confidence!) that while the textual variation between one edition and another is sometimes considerable, the physical difference between single copies within a single edition is inconsiderable. This statement is needed to explain what might otherwise appear to be an uneven balance in the bibliography as a whole.

For the reasons given above, normal procedures have been very slightly adapted to the special problems presented by Gissing's works. It is hoped that by this means the information which follows will be accessible both to bibliographer and bibliophiles on the one hand and to a wide range of literary people on the other. The list which follows corresponds to the order in which the details of a printed book are given throughout the bibliography and might therefore be read in conjunction with a sample description.

DATES

The date of publication only appears in the main entry if it is known from the evidence of the book or books being described. The entries in each part of the bibliography are in chronological order and an appendix provides the chronology of Gissing's work as a whole. Nonetheless, the absence of a date in a main description may mean, in the strict sense, that the date is not known.

TITLES

The title of the main entry is identical to that on the title page and will not correspond in all cases to the title on the spine or the title by which the book is popularly known.

COLLATION

Information under the subheading 'Collation' is given in the following order: (a) the signatures of gatherings or an indication of actual gatherings when there are no signatures; (b) the number of leaves; (c) the measurement in centimetres of the largest leaf in the book examined, the height being given first; (d) an abbreviated summary of the pagination which distinguishes between the text and the prelims, a summary included for convenience though it is, in effect, identical to what follows immediately under 'Contents.' Because it may happen that a reader has in his hands one volume only of a three-volume edition, the 'Collation' and 'Contents' are given for each volume separately.

CONTENTS

Information given under the subheading 'Contents' is to be distinguished from 'table of contents' in the book itself and constitutes the minimum transcription of those pages in a book which permit identification of it. It is a minimum description in a double sense. First, in transcribing the prelims one customarily moves closer to facsimile reproduction when the difficulty of distinguishing between one copy of a book and another is greatest. In the case of Gissing, this difficulty is not considerable. Second, except where it is essential, there is no detailed transcription of chapter headings, blank pages, and running titles in the body of the book described, because in the large number of copies examined no variations have been discovered.

CONTENTS IN DETAIL

So that a transcription under 'Contents' can be read easily and accurately, a number of minor points have to be made.

a Punctuation, except for the punctuation of what is transcribed, is reduced to the minimum.

b A colon invariably divides the *statement* about what is there on the page from the details of the *transcription* itself. (Thus: '[i] halftitle: WORKERS IN THE DAWN')

c To avoid clutter and to reduce the possibility of error the page number is used as the punctuation between items. (Thus: '[i] halftitle: WORKERS IN THE DAWN [ii] blank [iii] titlepage.') Any punctuations that falls between colons is transcribed from a copy of the book being described, except in the very rare case where the colon is part of what is being transcribed.

d The pagination of prelims where there are no numbers on the page derives from a backward count from the first numbered page of text, instances of the backward count not coinciding with the gathering or the actual numbers on some of the pages being duly noted.

e In works of more than one volume, items that are repeated are not re-transcribed. Thus, if the printer's imprint is to be found on the final page of each volume of a three-volume novel, it is transcribed in full under the sub-heading 'Contents' for Volume I, the word 'imprint' in the relevant place indicating that what is printed in Volumes II and III is in every respect identical.

f The existence of a table of contents is indicated simply by the word 'contents.' This means no more than that there is a page or more in the prelims in which a table of contents is given. Where the full transcription of the table of contents serves a purpose, it is given as a separate item which reports the prelim pages accurately, not the titles and page numbers of the text itself. The chapter headings in the content tables of the novels are, in the case of Gissing, without either bibliographical or critical interest: they are not therefore included.

BINDING VARIANTS

Of books published during Gissing's lifetime, books which therefore have a main entry in this bibliography, there are few genuine examples variant bindings.

Varient bindings of a few copies or of a single copy, and these indeed exist, come into a special category. Sometimes a trial binding was rejected in preference for something sturdier. Sometimes the author's presentation copies, usually six, were separately bound, as is conjectured must have been the case with *Workers in the Dawn*. Sometimes a contemporary rebinding of a book for its owner causes a search for a variant where in fact none exists. Such variants as exist are of course interesting in their own right and those that have been seen are described.

PART I

Works published during Gissing's lifetime

WORKERS IN THE DAWN

FIRST EDITION

WORKERS IN THE DAWN. / *A Novel.* / IN THREE VOLUMES. / BY / GEORGE R. GISSING. / [short rule] / VOL. I / [short rule] / *London:* / REMINGTON AND CO., / 5, ARUNDEL STREET, STRAND, W.C. / [short rule] / 1880. / [*All Rights Reserved.*]

VOLUME I

Collation [A]³B–2B⁸; 195 leaves (18.85 × 12.3); [i–vi] [1]–384

Contents [i] blank [ii] advertisement [iii] titlepage [iv] blank [v] contents [vi] blank [1]–384: END OF VOL. I. / [short rule] / Printed by REMINGTON & CO., 5, Arundel Street, Strand, W.C.

VOLUME II

Collation [A]³B–2C⁸2D²; 205 leaves (18.3 × 12.2); [i–vi] [1]–403 [404]

Contents [i] blank [ii] advertisement [iii] titlepage [iv] blank [v] contents [vi] blank [1]–403 text, on 403: END OF VOL. II. / [medium rule] / Printed by REMINGTON & CO., 5, Arundel Street, Strand W.C. [404] blank

VOLUME III

Collation [A]³B–2D⁸F2⁴2G²; 225 leaves (18.5 × 12.2); [i–vi] [1]–442 [443–4]

Contents [i] blank [ii] advertisement [iii] titlepage [iv] blank [v] contents [vi] blank [1]–442 text, on 442: THE END. / [medium rule] / Printed by REMINGTON & CO., 5, Arundel Street, Strand, W.C. [443–4] blank

Binding Spine, and boards at front and back, covered in olive-green cloth. Black coating on lining papers and recto of front free endpaper and verso of back free endpaper.

Front cover Near the top and bottom edges are two horizontal lines, below and above which run dotted black lines. In the space enclosed by these two borders is a rectangular frame. Above and below the top line of the frame run two lines from the right side to the left, not quite reaching the top left corner. Similarly, another pair of lines runs from bottom left towards right, again not quite reaching corner at right. Within the frame lines of varying length radiate towards the top. The design work on either side represents, on the right, a plant with leaves and flowers and on the left, a butterfly, the·two designs being joined by a horizontal line with an asterisk at its centre. Small scroll work designs are stamped about the top middle of the frame, one above and one below the upper line of frame. All design work on the front cover is stamped on in black.

Spine The line borders at top and bottom are extended over spine. At the top stamped in gilt: WORKERS / IN THE / DAWN / [short rule] / *GEORGE R.* / *GISSING* / VOL. I
Beneath this are two vertical parallel black lines with scroll work and at its lower end runs a horizontal black line extending the width of the spine. Between this black line and the lower lined border is stamped in gilt: REMINGTON

Back cover The two upper and lower black-lined borders are extended over to back cover. In the middle of cover is stamped in fancy black lettering: R

ALTERNATIVE BINDINGS

Remington gave Gissing the choice of five colours for the binding of *Workers in the Dawn*. In addition to the olive that Gissing chose, it appears that single copies were bound in green, scarlet, blue, and violet. Odd volumes of the violet and green bindings were in *NBL* reported to be in the possession of C.C. Kohler. The scarlet copy is in the Berg Collection and the blue in the Stark Library at Texas. These are not variant bindings in the strict sense, but rather pre-publication trial copies, of the kind that were frequently made, particularly when a book was being published at the author's expense.

PUBLICATION

During Gissing's first period in London, from the time that he arrived from the north of England in 1877 to the publication of *Workers in the Dawn* in 1880, he earned a living mostly by tutoring, but at the same time began a number of novels, completing a substantial part of at least one of them before turning to *Workers in the Dawn*. This he did in 1879. Although no record has survived of Gissing's day by day life in 1879, *Workers in the Dawn* was almost certainly written in three stages. The first ended in July when Gissing completed the early part of the novel where Lizzie Clinkscales was imagined as a major character in a simple story hinging upon a conflict between dedication to art and commitment to social reform (*Letters* 46, 47). Carrie Mitchell did not at this point exist. The second stage, which extended from August to November, involved the introduction of Carrie Mitchell whose presence as an entirely new main character gave the novel a psychological depth and interest it had previously lacked. A crucial stage had been reached by 20 August when

Gissing told his brother he had completed the twenty-eighth chapter. By 3 November the book was finished. 'It consists of 46 chapters, of some 450 MS pp, and will I fear, make three good volumes' (*Letters* 49). This statement is puzzling because the surviving MS has 709 pages, while 450 pages take the novel up to chapter 28, which is the point at which Carrie Mitchell was introduced. Either Gissing rewrote part of the novel in November after telling his brother he had finished it or he spent the same month converting a 450-page draft into a much longer fair copy. Whatever the explanation, Gissing sent a fair copy to Chatto & Windus, the first publisher he is known to have approached, early in December. The third stage extended from that date to the date of publication in March 1880, during which period he at some point, and almost certainly at the request of a publisher, revised the novel extensively in the manner described below.

From the *Letters* one gathers that *Workers in the Dawn* was turned down by at least four publishers during the early part of 1880: Chatto and Windus, Smith and Elder, Sampson Low, and Kegan Paul (*Letters* 52–3, 56, 57). In all probability he tried other publishers as well. Eventually he decided to spend what was left of his legacy on publishing the novel at his own expense and on 26 February 1880 signed the agreement with Remington, which is now in the Beinecke Library. The memorandum of agreement states: 'Our Reader's Report upon the MS mentioned in the margin being satisfactory, we whall be glad to undertake publication on the following terms: – a payment from you of £125 to be made in three instalments thus £50 on signing agreement £40 when first two volumes are printed and the balance of £35 when the 3rd Vol is printed. The work would be published in 3 vols at a guinea.' This arrangement is substantiated by the three receipts dated 1 March, 15 April, and 19 May, which are also in the Beinecke Library. The memorandum also specified that accounts were to be made up half-yearly and that Gissing was to receive two-thirds of the profits. Remington in fact printed 277 sets. Unfortunately the profits were not considerable. On 13 March 1881 Gissing told his brother that he was far from satisfied with Remington. 'I have at last heard from Remington, who sends me a cheque for *16 shillings*, Author's share of the proceeds up to last Christmas. He makes out that 49 copies have been sold, & £24 odd spent on advertising' (Pforzheimer). Gissing was to become very familiar with this experience during the next decade.

Workers in the Dawn was not republished during Gissing's lifetime, but in 1935 Doubleday Doran published it in two volumes, Robert Shafer editing it from a copy in which Volume I had considerable deletions and corrections in Gissing's hand. This copy he borrowed from its owner, Mrs Capra, as two letters in the Beinecke Library show. In the first letter, dated 21 July 1934 and addressed to R.T. Howey in Los Angeles, Professor Shafer asked for a complete, literal transcript of all the changes in the Capra copy since he had not been granted permission to see the original. In the second letter, dated 16 August 1934 and addressed to Mrs Capra c/o Frank Hooper at North River, Warren County, NY, he thanked her for copying out the corrections Gissing had made. There is no mention in these letters of there being or of there not being corrections to Volumes II and III, or even indeed any clear indication that Mr and Mrs Capra had Volumes II and III in their possession, although in his own preface Professor Shafer stated that only Volume I had been corrected.

No doubt this revision of *Workers in the Dawn* occurred in the early eighteen-nineties when Lawrence and Bullen encouraged Gissing to republish as many books as possible in single-volume format. Shafer indicated in his edition the corrections to the copy of the first edition on which it was based but did not feel justified in making the changes because he thought that the revision had not been completed. He avoided what he thought would be the anomaly of publishing a partially corrected text. Perhaps he was right. On the other hand, a good case could be made, on critical grounds, for the argument that Gissing did not correct Volumes II and III because there was no need. It must be noted that when Gissing engaged in this second revision, whether complete or incomplete, he did so without the original manuscript in front of him. No one since Robert Shafer has attempted to reconcile the two revisions and there is therefore a sense in which, despite a reprint of the first edition, the novel remains unpublished.

There is, however, a curiosity that ought to be noted. In 1930, the Bowling Green Press decided to make a new edition of *Workers in the Dawn* and invited a number of people, including George Moore, to write an introduction. After some delay, the introduction was written by Rebecca West and the novel printed and bound. Though copies exist, the edition was never published.

THE MANUSCRIPT

The manuscript of *Workers in the Dawn*, now in the Library of the Academic Center in the University of Texas, is a fair copy which carries the physical signs of its having been used in the print shop: it is divided up for setting and has the compositors' names in the margin. Though the three volumes have continuous pagination, there are many deletions not made in Gissing's normal way – that is, by near obliteration of the words by multiple lines – but by single or double horizontal strokes, which leave the deleted text virtually unscarred, so revealing that bowdlerization was made a condition of publication for a novel judged to be offensive. The equivalent of some fifty manuscript pages have been deleted from the MS. A letter from Gissing to his brother, Will, dated 11 March 1880, has confused the issue. In it he said: 'Remington wanted me to reduce the book, seeing that it would be vastly larger than the average novel of the day; but I told him that this would be impossible save by re-writing it, and so the printing goes ahead' (*Letters* 61). On the same day, however, he returned a batch of corrected proof to Remington, which makes it unlikely that he later changed his mind about the further revision of the book. This means that the revision of the manuscript as we now have it must have occurred before he told his brother that he would not revise. On the day he signed his contract with Remington, 26 February 1880, he had written to his brother, William: 'I have been working hard all day getting ready my first volume for the press, whither it goes at once' (*Letters* 60). Thus the most likely time for the revision of the manuscript is the period between the date earlier in February when Kegan Paul rejected the book and whenever Gissing knew that Remington would publish it.

II a

THE UNCLASSED

FIRST EDITION

THE UNCLASSED / A NOVEL / BY / GEORGE GISSING / AUTHOR OF 'WORKERS IN THE DAWN.' / 'Hast du nicht gute Gessellschaft gesehn? Es zeigt uns dein Büchein / Fast nur Gaukler und Volk, ja was noch neidriger ist. / Gute Gessellschaft hab'ich gesehn; man nennt sie die gute / Wenn sie zum kleinstein Gedicht keine Gelegenheit giebt.' – GOETHE. / *IN THREE VOLUMES. – VOL. I.* / LONDON: CHAPMAN AND HALL / LIMITED / 1884 / [*All rights reserved.*]

VOLUME I

Collation [A]⁴B–T⁸U⁶; 154 leaves (18.9 × 12.4); [i]–viii [1]–300

Contents [i] halftitle: THE UNCLASSED. / VOL. I. [ii] blank [iii] titlepage [iv] Bungay: CLAY AND TAYLOR, PRINTERS. [v] dedication: TO / M.C.R. [vi] blank [vii–viii] contents [1]–300 text, on 300: END OF VOL. I.

VOLUME II

Collation [A]³B–U⁸X⁶; 161 leaves (18.95 × 12.5); [i]–vi [1]–315 [316]

Contents [i] halftitle [ii] blank [iii] titlepage [iv] imprint [v]–vi contents [1]–315 text, on 315: END OF VOL. II. [316] blank

VOLUME III

Collation [A]³B–U⁸; 155 leaves (18.9×12.4); [i]–vi [1]–304

Contents [i] halftitle [ii] blank [iii] titlepage [iv] imprint [v]–vi contents [1]–304 text, on 304: THE END. / [short rule] / CLAY AND TAYLOR, PRINTERS, BUNGAY, SUFFOLK. S. & H.

Binding Spine, and boards at front and back, covered in dark blue-green cloth. Yellow coating on lining papers, and recto of front free endpaper and verso of back free endpaper.

Front cover Within a frame of three parallel lines and stamped in black a floral border on band extends, at centre, over the left hand edge to the spine.

Spine Stamped in gilt: THE / UNCLASSED / [rule stamped in black] / VOL. I / CHAPMAN & HALL

Back cover Plain except for publisher's monogram blind-stamped at centre.

II b

SECOND EDITION

THE UNCLASSED / BY / GEORGE GISSING / 'Hast du nicht gute Gessellschaft gesehn? Es zeigt uns dein Buchlein / Fast nur Gaukler und Volk, ja was noch neidriger ist. / Gute Gessellschaft hab'ich gesehn; man nennt sie de gute / Wenn sie zum kleinstein Gedicht keine Gelegenheit giebt.' / – GOETHE / [publisher's stamp] / NEW EDITION / LONDON / LAWRENCE AND BULLEN / 16 HENRIETTA STREET, COVENT GARDEN, W.C. / 1895

Collation [π]⁴A–T⁸U⁴; 160 leaves (19×12); [i–vi] vii–viii [1]–312

Contents [i] halftitle: THE UNCLASSED [ii] publisher's advertisement [iii]titlepage [iv] imprint: *Printed by* BALLANTYNE, HANSON & CO / *At the Ballantyne Press* [v] preface [vi] blank vii–viii contents [1]–312 text, on 312: *Printed by* BALLANTYNE, HANSON & CO. / *Edinburgh and London*

Binding Spine, and boards at front and back, covered in maroon cloth. Endpapers very dark green.

Front cover Plain.

Spine Stamped in gilt and with the title and the name of the publisher enclosed in a simple rectangle: THE / UNCLASSED / GEORGE / GISSING / LAWRENCE & BULLEN

Back cover Plain.

Advertisements In most copies 32 pages of separately paginated advertisements are sewn in; the notice of Gissing's work corresponds to the advertisement on [ii] of the book itself. Five novels in addition to *The Unclassed* are advertised in a single volume edition to be sold at 6/-: *Eve's Ransom*, *In the Year of Jubilee*, *The Odd Women*, *Denzil Quarrier*, and *The Emancipated*.

II c

AMERICAN STEREOTYPE OF SECOND EDITION

The second edition was published in North America by R.F. Fenno. The text is identical to that of the second edition, the only significant difference being the prelims. The titlepage is as follows:
[medium double rule] / The Unclassed / [medium rule] / BY GEORGE GISSING / *Author of* 'The Odd Women,' 'Eve's Ransom,' / 'In the Year of Jubilee,' 'The Whirlpool,' Etc., Etc. / [medium rule] / 'Hast du nicht gute Gessellschaft gesehn? Es zeigt uns dein Buchlein / Fast nur Gaukler und Volk, ja was noch niedriger ist. / Gute Gessellschaft hab'ich gesehn; man nennt sie de gute / Wenn sie zum kleinstein Gedicht keine Gelegenheit giebt.' / – GOETHE / [medium rule] / [publisher's stamp] [medium rule] / R.F. FENNO & COMPANY / 9 & 11 EAST SIXTEENTH STREET, NEW YORK / [medium double rule]
The imprint in the prelims is: COPYRIGHT, 1896 / R.F. FENNO & COMPANY
The American issue was bound in brown cloth and, according to *GGB*, was also issued in wrappers.

RE-ISSUES

The second edition of *The Unclassed* appeared as part of Bell's 'Indian and Colonial Library.'

PUBLICATION

After the publication of *Workers in the Dawn*, Gissing made a number of false starts on new novels. One of these, *A Son of the Age*, was half finished but never completed. Another, *Mrs. Grundy's Enemies*, was finished and accepted by Bentley, but not in the end published. In 1882 Helen was committed to an invalid's home in Battersea and for the next eight or nine years Gissing lived alone. Not much is known about the writing of *The Unclassed*, but in all likelihood it was started early in 1883, Bentley having accepted *Mrs. Grundy's Enemies* on 26 December 1882. In a letter to his brother dated 8 December 1883 he announced: 'New novel will be finished on Tuesday. I send it to Chapman & Hall. The name is *The Unclassed*' (*Letters* 135).

Chapman & Hall paid Gissing £30 for the lease of the copyright for a three year period, Gissing to retain the copyright subsequently (*Adams*) and to receive a 5/- royalty on each copy sold after the first impression of 400 (*Notebook*). The typed agreement between Gissing and Chapman & Hall, dated 13 March 1884, is in the Beinecke.

Gissing often said that he wished to forget this novel which derived from one of his blackest and loneliest years. To Bertz, for example, on 11 September 1889: 'Heavens! how it must have brought back old days, to reread *Workers* and *The Unclassed*! Not for any consideration would I open those dreadful books! All I have ever written seems to be apprentice work; I fear to examine it!' (*Bertz* 73). Later, when he was telling Bertz about the possibility of its being reissued, he said he found it difficult to associate himself with his own early days. 'And how strange a thing it is when, in walking about the streets of London, I pass the streets where I lived in those days of misery! Of course *that man* and *I* are not identical. He is a relation of mine, who died long ago; that's all' (*Bertz* 191).

Nevertheless he did revise the book for Lawrence & Bullen and the considerably shortened version, the second edition described above, appeared in 1895 in one volume. According to *NBL* this was reissued in 1901 by A.H. Bullen.

III a

ISABEL CLARENDON

FIRST EDITION

ISABEL CLARENDON / BY / GEORGE GISSING / In Two Volumes. / VOL. I. / 'C'était plus qu'une vie, hélas! c'était un monde / Qui s'était effacé!' / LONDON: / CHAPMAN AND HALL, / LIMITED. / 1886

VOLUME I

Collation $A^2B-T^8U^3$; 149 leaves (18.65×12.5); [i–iv] [1]–293 [294]

Contents [i] halftitle: ISABEL CLARENDON. [ii] blank [iii] titlepage [iv] imprint: CHARLES DICKENS AND EVANS, / CRYSTAL PALACE PRESS. [1]–293 text, on 293: END OF VOL. I. / [short rule] / CHARLES DICKENS AND EVANS, CRYSTAL PALACE PRESS. [294] blank

VOLUME II

Collation A²B–X⁸Y⁴; 166 leaves (18.6×12.5); [i–iv] [1]–328

Contents [i] halftitle [ii] blank [iii] titlepage [iv] imprint [1]–328 text, on 328: THE END. / [short rule] / CHARLES DICKENS AND EVANS, CRYSTAL PALACE PRESS

Binding Spine, and boards at front and back, covered in dark green cloth. Endpapers of patterned light green and white on white spotted light green background; regular, repeated motifs of bird and flowers, and leaves and swirling sprigs (birds and flowers in white outlined in green, leaves and stems in green and outlined in white). Also on recto of front free endpaper and verso of back free endpaper.

Front cover Stamped in black at top and bottom a thin horizontal border and at the centre a wider border with a design.

Spine The two black lines at top and bottom are extended over spine. Similarly the border along the middle. Stamped in gilt: ISABEL / CLARENDON / [short rule] / *GEORGE GISSING* / [short rule] / VOL. I. / CHAPMAN & HALL

Back cover Publisher's monogram stamped in black at centre.

PUBLICATION

The first version of *Isabel Clarendon*, the weakest and most uninteresting of Gissing's early novels, was written during the winter of 1884–5, as is demonstrated by the frequent references to the novel in *Letters*. 'The task of getting into the fictitious world one has created always costs agony', he told his brother on 18 September 1884, in a remark which presumably indicates that he was just settling down to real work on the book (*Letters* 148). He worked on through the winter, moving in December to The Cornwall Residences – his home until he remarried, and late in March reported that, after 'toiling incessantly,' the book which was still called *The Lady of Knightswell* was at last finished. Korg's remark that '*Isabel Clarendon* was written expressly for Meredith' is quite misleading, since, as Pierre Coustillas has suggested in his introduction to the photographic reproduction of the first edition issued in 1969, the character of the novel owes much more to Gissing's new friends, the Glaussons and their circle. The task of getting into the fictitious world of *Isabel Clarendon* was in fact so agonizing that Meredith, as Chapman and Hall's reader, told Gissing that the book would have to be rewritten.

Gissing accepted this advice, spent the greater part of June and July 1885 rewriting it in two volumes, renamed it *Isabel Clarendon* and in a gloomy letter to his brother on 9 August 1885 announced that he had finished. 'Tonight I finish *Isabel Clarendon*. I have done my best to make the story as realistic as possible. The ending is as unromantic as could be, and several threads are left to hang loose; for even so it is in real life; you cannot gather up and round off each person's story. But this time I believe the work to be good. Yesterday I wrote for nine hours, and at last in that peculiar excitement in which one cannot see the paper and pen, but only the words' (*Letters* 164). Even at this point, however, it is possible that his labours had not ended. Retrospectively he entered in the *Diary* the dates of July–September 1885 for *Isabel Clarendon*, and it is just possible that the slight disturbance in the MS, which is a fair copy of this second version of the book, represents further work done either before or after he had resubmitted it to Chapman and Hall.

Whatever the novel's quality, there is no doubt that Chapman & Hall treated Gissing shabbily over *Isabel Clarendon*. According to the *Notebook*, though by verbal agreement he was to have received half the profits, he in fact received nothing. And by the time the novel appeared in June 1886, Gissing had written his way back, as it were, into the main line of his development. *Isabel Clarendon* was an unfortunate digression.

Pierre Coustillas has shown that Gissing began the process of revision for a one-volume edition proposed by A.H. Bullen in the early nineties and has identified the copy, now in the Alexander Turnbull Library in Wellington, New Zealand, which Gissing probably used. Gissing never completed the work, however, having as little enthusiasm for a new edition of *Isabel Clarendon* as for *Workers in the Dawn*.

THE MANUSCRIPT

The manuscript of *Isabel Clarendon*, which is a fair copy of the revised version of the book, is in the Pforzheimer Library. It is a remarkably clean copy, the only significant disturbance of the text being the omission of 3 MS pages from each of the two volumes.

IV a

DEMOS

FIRST EDITION

DEMOS / *A STORY OF ENGLISH SOCIALISM* / [short rule] / 'Jene machen Partei; welch' unerlaubtes Beginnen! / Aber unsre Partei, freilich, versteht sich von selbst' / GOETHE / [short rule] / IN THREE VOLUMES /

VOL. I. / LONDON / SMITH, ELDER, & CO., 15 WATERLOO PLACE / 1886 / [*All rights reserved*]

VOLUME I

Collation [A]²B–U⁸X⁶; 160 leaves (18.7×12.6); [i–iv] [1]–315 [316]

Contents [i] halftitle: DEMOS / VOL. I. [ii] blank [iii] titlepage [iv] blank [1]–315 text, on 315: END OF THE FIRST VOLUME. / PRINTED BY / SPOTTISWOODE AND CO., NEW-STREET SQUARE / LONDON [316] blank

VOLUME II

Collation [A]²B–T⁸U⁴; 150 leaves (18.75×12.6); [i–iv] [1]–296

Contents [i] halftitle [ii] blank [iii] titlepage [iv] blank [1]–296 text, on 296; END OF THE SECOND VOLUME. / [short rule] / *Spottiswoode & Co., Printers, New-Street Square, London*

VOLUME III

Collation [A]²B–T⁸U⁴; 150 leaves (18.75×12.65); [i–iv] [1]–295 [296]

Contents [i] halftitle [ii] blank [iii] titlepage [iv] blank [1]–295 text, on 295: THE END. / [short rule] / *Spottiswoode & Co. Printers, New-Street Square, London.* [296] blank

Binding Spine, and boards at front and back, covered in coffee brown cloth. Purple coating on lining papers and on recto of front free endpapers and verso of back free endpapers.

Front cover The design work of the front cover is stamped in black and consists of a rectangular frame (a wide border at top and bottom and horizontal parallel lines at either margin), the space within being divided into alternate squares and rectangles. Within each square is a daisy-shaped flower. Within each rectangle, a circle and two dots. Blind-stamped on the lower border is a motif of eight-petalled flowers and dots. Across the middle of the cover, also stamped in black, is the title: DEMOS

Spine The same top and bottom borders extend over the spine. At the top, below the border, is stamped in gilt: DEMOS / A TALE OF / ENGLISH / SOCIALISM and at the bottom, just above the lower border, also in gilt: SMITH ELDER & CO.

Back cover Plain.

Variant binding Spine, and boards at front and back, covered in dark jungle green cloth. Yellow coating on lining papers and on recto of front free endpaper and verso of back free endpaper.

Front cover Same design as other copy, but the design work R and letterings are dark purple in colour.

Spine As copy 1 except for colour of binding.

Back cover As copy 1 except for colour of binding.

IV b

SECOND EDITION

DEMOS / A STORY OF ENGLISH SOCIALISM / BY / GEORGE GISSING / AUTHOR OF 'THYRZA' ETC. / [short rule] / 'Jene machen Partei; welch' unerlaubtes Beginnen! / Aber unsre Partei, freilich, versteht sich von selbst' / GOETHE / [short rule] / *A NEW EDITION* / LONDON / SMITH, ELDER, & CO., 15 WATERLOO PLACE / 1886 / [*All rights reserved*]

Collation [A]²B–Z⁸AA–HH⁸; 242 leaves (19×12.5); [i–iv] [1]–477 [478–80]

Contents [i] halftitle: A STORY / OF / ENGLISH SOCIALISM [ii] blank [iii] titlepage [iv] blank [1]–477 text, on 477: THE END. / PRINTED BY SPOTTISWOODE AND CO., NEW-STREET SQUARE / LONDON [478] blank [479–80] advertisements

Binding Spine, and boards at front and back, covered in brown cloth. Endpapers plain.

Front cover Half a centimetre from top and bottom is a border, stamped in black, consisting of two lines within which is a band with a very simple floral pattern. At centre, stamped in black, a stylized flower.

Spine The borders are continued from the front cover to the spine. Above and below each border is an additional gilt line. Stamped in gilt: DEMOS. / THE AUTHOR OF / THYRZA. / SMITH, ELDER & CO.

Back cover The borders, blind-stamped, are continued from the front cover. Otherwise plain.

Errata slip Between [iv] and [1] an errata slip has been pasted in. It reads: *Errata.* / Page 42, line 21, *for* cheap reprints *of* translations, *read* cheap reprints *or* translations. / Demos. 1 vol.

IV c

REISSUE OF SECOND EDITION

DEMOS / A STORY OF ENGLISH SOCIALISM / BY / GEORGE GISSING / AUTHOR OF 'THYRZA' 'THE NETHER WORLD' ETC. / [short rule] / 'Jene machen Partei: welch' unerlaubtes Beginnen! / Aber unsre Partei, freilich, versteht sich von selbst' / GOETHE / [short rule] / *A NEW EDITION* / LONDON / SMITH, ELDER, & CO., 15 WATERLOO PLACE / 1888 / *All rights reserved*

Collation [A]²B–GG⁸HH⁶; 241 leaves (17.2 × 11.55); [i–iv] [1]–477 [478]

Contents [i] halftitle: A STORY / OF / ENGLISH SOCIALISM [ii] advertisement of other novels by Gissing [iii] titlepage [iv] blank [1]–477 text, on 477: THE END. / PRINTED BY / SPOTTISWOODE AND CO., NEW-STREET SQUARE / LONDON [478] blank

Binding Spine, and boards at front and back, bound in bright red cloth. Cream endpapers.

Front cover Near the top edge runs a border formed by two narrow black lines about 1.27 cms apart, enclosing within them a black band with an embossed chain pattern in red running through; beneath this is another black band bordered by black lines and with the title embossed in red: DEMOS. Between the border at the top and an identical border at the bottom is stamped in black: AUTHOR OF / 'THE NETHER WORLD'

Spine The borders at top and bottom are extended over the spine. At the top is stamped in gilt: DEMOS / BY / GEORGE / GISSING and at the bottom: SMITH ELDER & C°

Back cover Plain except for the two borders at the top and bottom.

PUBLICATION

Demos was written during the winter of 1885–6 after a number of false starts. In June 1884 Gissing had told Algernon that he was poised to write a new novel: 'It is to be called *Demos*' (*Berg*). And on 2 August 1885 he announced: 'I am working hard at the first chapters of my new book *Demos*' (*Letters* 160). Yet as far as one can judge, it was not until November of that year that he really settled down to work. On 4 November he said once again that he would begin the book, another reminder of the fact that when Gissing told someone that he was beginning a book he meant only that, in a physical sense, he was at chapter one, page one. The early labour on what he called 'rather a savage satire on working class aims and capacities' proceeded slowly, and by the time that he wrote the frequently quoted letter to Ellen, dated 22 November 1885, he had still only written a third of the first volume, 'with much toil and endless re-writing' (*Letters* 174). He firmly intended to finish the book by the spring, however, and in this he succeeded, for he returned the last batch of corrected proofs on 14 March 1886. Perhaps because he described minutely people and conditions which, though unfamiliar to many of his readers, were nonetheless of current interest, and yet did so in a detached and unsympathetic way, the book enjoyed an immediate success. It was successful from the point of view of the publisher, that is to say, but not for Gissing himself, since he had sold the copyright to Smith, Elder for £100.

The standard practice of Smith, Elder, at least as far as Gissing's work was concerned, was to republish a novel in single volume form, unless it had failed completely, and then reissue from the same plates as demand warranted. Normally there would be a 6/- edition, followed by a reissue at 3/6, this followed in turn by an issue in limp red cloth at 2/6 and a 'yellowback' at 2/-. In the case of *Demos*, the second edition in one volume appeared in November 1886 and it was then reissued both in the original format and in the 3/6, 2/6, and 2/- formats in 1888. The first American edition, which appeared as No. 522 of Harper's Franklin Square Library, and the two-volume edition by Tauchnitz, were both based on the second edition and appeared in 1886. Thus only the first edition is of textual importance. Despite the success of *Demos*, however, Gissing himself only found out about the various reissues by accident. He noted in the *Diary*, for example, that he had seen a copy priced at 3/6 and on another occasion that he had read the advertisement for the 2/- reprint.

On the various occasions when a collected edition was mooted, Smith, Elder declined to part with the copyright and indeed not only continued to issue the novel in single volume form during Gissing's lifetime (1890, 1892, 1897) but also after his death (1908), their interest being sustained until the business was taken over by Murray. Smith, Elder's papers did not survive the Hitler war but it seems reasonable to suppose that *Demos* was enough of a success commercially for Smith, Elder to speculate with four more novels, only one of them, *New Grub Street*, being of anything like the same quality.

It should be said that in each case the same publishing procedure was adopted though there were physical differences between the five novels. Thus, Smith, Elder published one-volume second editions of *Demos*, *Thyrza*, *A Life's Morning*, *The Nether World*, and *New Grub Street* on good paper, with a stout binding and a page size of approximately 18.5 × 12.5, for sale at 6/- each, but some were bound in brown and some in maroon cloth on boards and there were incidental variations of design. Similarly they were all reissued, from the same plates, in the 3/6, 2/6, and 2/- formats. The 3/6 reissue can be identified by the smaller page size of approximately 16.5 × 11 within boards, usually bound in maroon cloth. The 2/6 reissue, with a page size of 17.3 × 11.4 is bound in limp red cloth. And the 2/- reissue, or yellowback, is in boards with a printed pictorial design on the front cover. Smith, Elder had in short a

The Novels of Gissing Published by Smith, Elder & Co.

TITLE	SERIAL	FIRST EDITION IN 3 VOLUMES	REISSUE OF FIRST EDITION IN 3 VOLUMES	I VOL. AT 6/-	I VOL. AT 3/6	I VOL. AT 2/6	I VOL. AT 2/-	US EDITIONS	TAUCHNITZ REPRINTS	TRANSLATION	REVISION
DEMOS pp 34-40		1886		1886	1888	1888	1888	Harper 1886	1886	In French: Hachette 1888, by F. le Breton. In German: 1892, by Clara Steinitz	Not revised by Gissing. Copy-text is the first edition.
THYRZA pp 40-4		1887		1891	1892	1892	1892				Revised extensively by Gissing. Copy-text is the 2nd edition of 1891.
A LIFE'S MORNING pp 44-6	*The Cornhill* Jan.-Dec. 1888	1888		1889	1889	1889	1889	J. B. Lippincott 1888			Not revised. Gissing corrected proof for both serial and first edition.
THE NETHER WORLD pp 46-8		1889		1889	1890	1890	1890	Harper 1889			Unrevised
NEW GRUB STREET pp 53-4		1891	1891	1891	1892	1892	1892		1891	In French 1911. In German: 1892, by Adele Berger	Revised by Gissing for Gabrielle Fleury's translation

(See introduction, p 13 ff and the *Demos* entry pp 13-15 for more detailed statements on the Smith, Elder reissues.)

standard practice, though as indicated above the result, in the case of Gissing, is not a uniform edition but a collection of one-volume second editions and reissues from them, the relations between them being instantly recognizable when the books are gathered together. The preceding table is designed to simplify the reading of the five Smith, Elder entries in this bibliography, that is entries IV, V, VI, VII, and IX. Though the 3/6, 2/6, and 2/- version of each of the Smith, Elder novels are only reissues, the complete run is given descriptively in the *New Grub Street* entry (see IX, pp 53–9).

THE MANUSCRIPT

The manuscript of *Demos* is now in the Berg Collection in the New York Public Library. It is a fair copy bound in one volume but paginated consistently in three volumes which correspond to the three volumes of the printed text (volume I [1]–121; volume II [1]–121; volume III [1]–120). The manuscript does not appear to be of critical interest, though in volume III the physical disturbance shows that a chapter, originally chapter III, has been omitted.

V a

THYRZA

FIRST EDITION

THYRZA / *A TALE* / BY / GEORGE GISSING / AUTHOR OF 'DEMOS' / ETC. / [short rule] / ἄμμες δὲ βροτοὶ οἵδε·βροτοὺς βροτοὶ αειδωμες / IN THREE VOLUMES / VOL. I / LONDON / SMITH, ELDER, & CO., 15 WATERLOO PLACE / 1887 / [*All rights reserved*]

VOLUME I

Collation [A]⁴B–T⁸U²; 150 leaves (18.75 × 12.7); [i–viii] [1]–291 [292]

Contents [i–ii] blank [iii] halftitle: THYRZA / VOL. I. [iv] blank [v] titlepage [vi] blank [vii] contents [viii] blank [1]–291 text, on 291: END OF THE FIRST VOLUME / PRINTED BY / SPOTTISWOODE AND CO., NEW-STREET SQUARE / LONDON [292] blank

VOLUME II

Collation [A]⁴B–U⁸X⁶; 162 leaves (18.7 × 12.7); [i–viii] [1]–316

Contents [i–ii] blank [iii] halftitle [iv] blank [v] titlepage [vi] blank [vii] contents [viii] blank [1]–316 text, on 316: END OF THE SECOND VOLUME / PRINTED BY / SPOTTISWOODE AND CO., NEW-STREET SQUARE / LONDON

VOLUME III

Collation [A]⁴B–T⁸U⁴X²; 154 leaves (18.75 × 12.65); [i–viii] [1]–298 [299–300]

Contents [i–ii] blank [iii] halftitle [iv] blank [v] titlepage [vi] blank [vii] contents [viii] blank [1]–298 text, on 298: THE END. / PRINTED BY / SPOTTISWOODE AND CO., NEW-STREET SQUARE / LONDON [299–300] publisher's advertisement

Binding Spine, and boards at front and back, covered in a reddish brown cloth. Black coating on lining papers and recto and verso of front and back free endpapers respectively.

Front cover Between two decorative borders stamped in black at top and bottom: THYRZA

Spine Between the borders at top and bottom which are carried over from the front cover and stamped in gilt: THYRZA / BY THE / AUTHOR OF / 'DEMOS' / [two short dashes] / VOL. I. / SMITH, ELDER & CO.

Back cover Plain.

V b

SECOND EDITION

THYRZA / A TALE / BY / GEORGE GISSING / AUTHOR OF 'DEMOS' 'THE NETHER WORLD' ETC. / *A NEW EDITION* / LONDON / SMITH, ELDER, & CO., 15 WATERLOO PLACE / 1891 / [*All rights reserved*]

Collation [A]⁴B–Z⁸AA–HH⁸II⁴KK²; 250 leaves (18.5 × 12.2); [i–viii] [1]–490 [491–2]

Contents [i–ii] blank [iii] halftitle: THYRZA [iv] advertisement [v] titlepage [vi] blank [vii–viii (numbered vi)] contents [1]–490 text, on 490: THE END / PRINTED BY / SPOTTISWOODE AND CO., NEW-STREET SQUARE / LONDON [491–2] advertisement

Binding Spine, and boards at front and back, covered in mustard brown cloth. Endpapers plain.

Front cover Stamped in black, a 2-centimetre wide band at top and bottom, with floral design. Stylized flower stamped in black at centre.

Spine Band, stamped in black, continued from front cover at top and bottom. Between: THYRZA / [short rule] / A TALE / GEORGE / GISSING / SMITH, ELDER & CO.

Back cover Band at top and bottom, blind-stamped, continued from spine. Otherwise plain.

V c

REISSUE OF SECOND EDITION

THYRZA / A TALE / BY / GEORGE GISSING / AUTHOR OF 'DEMOS' 'THE NETHER WORLD' ETC. / *A NEW EDITION* / LONDON / SMITH, ELDER & CO., 15 WATERLOO PLACE / 1892 / [*All rights reserved*]

Collation [A]⁴B–HH⁸II⁴KK⁸; 256 leaves (17.4 × 11.4); [a–b] [i]–vi [1]–490 [491–504]

Contents [a–b] blank [i] halftitle: THYRZA [ii] advertisement of other novels by Gissing [iii] titlepage [iv] blank [v]–vi contents [1]–490 text, on 490: THE END. / PRINTED BY / SPOTTISWOODE AND CO., NEW-STREET SQUARE / LONDON [491–504] publisher's advertisement, at the foot of each page: [long double rule] / London: SMITH, ELDER, & CO., 15 Waterloo Place.

Binding Spine, and boards at front and back, bound in bright red cloth. Yellow coating on lining papers and recto of front free endpaper and verso of back free endpaper.

Front cover Near the top edge runs a border which consists of two narrow black lines enclosing within them a black band with an embossed chain pattern in red running through. Beneath this is another black band, bordered by black lines and with the title embossed in red: .THYRZA.

Then, stamped in black: BY / GEORGE GISSING / AUTHOR OF / 'THE NETHER WORLD' Near the bottom edge the same border as that at the top is repeated.

Spine Between the borders at top and bottom which are extended over from the spine and stamped in gilt: THYRZA / BY / GEORGE / GISSING / SMITH ELDER & CO.

Back cover Plain except for the two borders.

PUBLICATION

Thyrza demonstrates in miniature the process by which Gissing arrived at the form of a novel that was artistically acceptable at least to him. He wrote it in a hurry and revised it at leisure. There is no point in thinking of an author that he should have done this or that: he works in the way he has to work. Gissing simply falls into that class of writer who sees things in a book after publication which other people might have seen at an earlier stage. At all events it is here the second edition which provides the definitive text.

On 28 April 1886 he wrote to his sister, Margaret: 'I am toiling fearfully over the construction of a new book, and fear that I shall not begin the actual writing for a week or so yet. I have got to go over a hat factory, a lunatic asylum, and other strange places; also to wander much in the slums' (*Letters* 179). About this book he writes to his family fairly frequently, for it does indeed become a toil. By July he is well into the first volume but proceeding slowly. 'I am living at present in Lambeth, doing my best to get at the meaning of that strange world, so remote from our civilization' (*Letters* 182). In fact he was to write the first volume seven times before he had finished it. 'I have a book in my head,' he wrote on the last day of July, 'which no-one else can write, a book which will contain the very spirit of London working-class life' (*Letters* 184). After a holiday break in the early autumn which he spent on the south coast, mostly in Eastbourne, he wrote the last part of the novel 'with fever and delight' and on 15 January 1887 announced its completion. '*Thyrza* was finished yesterday morning. Thyrza herself is one of the most beautiful dreams I ever had or shall have. I value the book really more than anything I have yet done. The last chapters drew many tears. I shall be glad when you know *Thyrza* and her sister. The vulgar will not care for them, I expect' (*Letters* 189).

Smith, Elder valued the book sufficiently highly to offer Gissing a choice of terms: either a 15 per cent royalty on each copy sold, the first printing to consist of 500 copies, or the outright purchase of the copyright for £100. Gissing chose the latter. (The subsequent sale of the copyright for £10 is discussed briefly in the introduction.)

Gissing revised *Thyrza* during the early part of 1891. On 31 January 1891 he noted in the *Diary* that he had received a copy from Smith, Elder and on 5 March he told Bertz that he had finished the work. '*Thyrza* I have corrected and greatly abbreviated; I hope the thing is improved' (*Bertz* 118). The 6/- edition in fact appeared in the summer of 1891 and from it Smith, Elder produced cheaper reissues in their normal manner, those costing 3/6 and 2/- bearing the date of 1892.

THE MANUSCRIPT

The manuscript of *Thyrza*, now in the Huntington, carries the notation: 'Written from May 1886 to Jan 1887.' It is a fair copy which has been divided up for use by compositors, their names indicating that two separate teams were used. The pagination shows that a few changes of arrangement were made at the last moment.

Volume I   [1]-52, 54-103, 104-10 (this last group being the original beginning of Volume II)

Volume II 1–106 (1–85 are renumbered, having previously been 8–92)
Volume III 1–106

Throughout the manuscript there are occasional deletions of a few lines at a time.

VI a

A LIFE'S MORNING

FIRST EDITION

A LIFE'S MORNING / BY / GEORGE GISSING / AUTHOR OF 'DEMOS' 'THYRZA' ETC / *IN THREE VOLUMES* / VOL. I. / LONDON / SMITH, ELDER, & CO., 15 WATERLOO PLACE / 1888 / [*All rights reserved*]

VOLUME I

Collation [A]⁴B–U⁸X⁴Y²; 162 leaves (18.9 × 12.7); [i–viii] [1]–315 [316]

Contents [i–ii] blank [iii] halftitle [iv] blank [v] titlepage [vi] blank [vii] contents [viii] blank [1]–315 text, on 315: END OF THE FIRST VOLUME. / PRINTED BY / SPOTTISWOODE AND CO., NEW-STREET SQUARE / LONDON [316] blank

VOLUME II

Collation [A]⁴B–U⁸; 156 leaves (18.9 × 12.75); [i–viii] [1]–303 [304]

Contents [i–ii] blank [iii] halftitle [iv] blank [v] titlepage [vi] blank [vii] contents [viii] blank [1]–303 text, on 303: END OF THE SECOND VOLUME. / PRINTED BY / SPOTTISWOODE AND CO., NEW-STREET SQUARE / LONDON [304] blank

VOLUME III

Collation [A]⁴B–Y⁸; 172 leaves (18.85 × 12.7); [i–viii] [1]–333 [334–6]

Contents [i–ii] blank [iii] halftitle [iv] blank [v] titlepage [vi] blank [vii] contents [viii] blank [1]–333 text, on 333: THE END. / PRINTED BY SPOTTISWOODE AND CO., NEW-STREET SQUARE / LONDON [334] blank [335–6] publisher's advertisement

Binding Spine, and boards at front and back, covered in brick brown cloth. Yellow coating on lining papers and recto and verso of front and back endpapers respectively.

Front cover Except for a 2.5 cms wide margin on the left and triangular shapes at the two outer corners, the cloth binding has a mottled effect. The other areas, though of the same piece of cloth, are of a smooth texture. At each junction where the two textures meet is a pair of narrow black lines.

Spine Stamped in black at top and bottom a double border between which, stamped in gilt: A / LIFE'S / MORNING / [short rule] VOL. I / GEORGE / GISSING / SMITH, ELDER & CO.

Back cover Identical to front cover, except that the smooth textured margin is now on the right.

VI b

SECOND EDITION

A LIFE'S MORNING / BY / GEORGE GISSING / AUTHOR OF 'DEMOS' 'THYRZA' ETC. / *A NEW EDITION* / LONDON / SMITH, ELDER, & CO., 15 WATERLOO PLACE / 1889 / [*All rights reserved*]

Collation [A]²B–Y⁸Z⁶; 176 leaves (17 × 11); [i–iii] iv [1]–348

Contents [i] titlepage [ii] blank [iii]–iv contents [1]–348 text, on 348: PRINTED BY / SPOTTISWOODE AND CO., NEW-STREET SQUARE / LONDON

Binding Paper on boards, with printed designs.

Front cover A black rectangle covers all but a narrow margin of the front cover. This rectangle itself has a margin consisting of a single red line at either side and a double red line at top and bottom. At each corner where the lines intersect are six small red dots. At the centre is a large (10.8 × 8.4) coloured representation of a man and woman meeting in a wood. Above the picture are the words: PRICE TWO SHILLINGS / *A Life's Morning* [black letter] Below the picture: By George Gissing [black letter] / Author of 'Demos' 'Thyrza' &c [black letter / LONDON: SMITH. ELDER. & CO.

Spine The spine is divided into ornamental bands printed in the same colours as the front cover, except that the title and the name of the author are given prominence by being printed on a white rectangle. The words on the spine are: A LIFE'S / MORNING / [short rule] / GEORGE GISSING / Two / Shillings / Smith Elder / and Co

Back cover Printed in black on the back cover is a full-paged, double column listing of 'CHEAP EDITIONS OF POPULAR WORKS' published by Smith, Elder, & Co.

PUBLICATION

According to the letters Gissing started to write *A Life's Morning* in August 1885 (*Letters* 168), though in the *Diary* he noted that it had been written between September and November of that year. Despite the fact that Smith, Elder liked it, there were snags to be overcome including, according to Roberts, the request that Gissing should rewrite the ending. Eventually it was published in serial form in the *Cornhill* in twelve monthly instalments between January and December 1888 and in book form on 15 November 1888 (*Diary*) in what, for Gissing and Smith, Elder, was a normal edition of 500 copies. *Adams* confirms that Gissing received £50 for the serial and £50 for the book.

Probably as soon as it was written and certainly by the time it was published, Gissing recognized *A Life's Morning* as one of his weaker works. The *Diary*, with the mention of his having received proofs to correct at two quite different times, perhaps provides the clue to the fact that he revised it. If so the novel cannot have been very satisfactory when he wrote it hurriedly in 1885 before beginning *Demos*. With *Isabel Clarendon*, *A Life's Morning* has to be regarded as apprentice work.

VII a

THE NETHER WORLD

FIRST EDITION

THE / NETHER WORLD / *A NOVEL* / BY / GEORGE GISSING / AUTHOR OF 'DEMOS,' ETC. / 'La peinture d'un fumier peut être justifiée pourvu qu'il y pousse une / belle fleur; sans cela, le fumier n'est que repoussant.' / M. RENAN, *at the Académie Française, Feb. 21, 1889.* / IN THREE VOLS. / VOL. I / LONDON / SMITH, ELDER, & CO., 15 WATERLOO PLACE / 1889

VOLUME I

Collation $[\pi]^4$A–S^{8}T^2; 150 leaves (18.9 × 12.7); [i–viii] [1]–291 [292]

Contents [i–ii] blank [iii] halftitle [iv] imprint: PRINTED BY BALLANTYNE, HANSON AND CO. / EDINBURGH AND LONDON. [v] titlepage [vi] blank [vii] contents [viii] blank [1]–291 text, on 291: END OF VOL I / [short rule] / PRINTED BY BALLANTYNE, HANSON AND CO. / EDINBURGH AND LONDON [292] blank

VOLUME II

Collation [A]–T^{8}U^4; 156 leaves (18.9 × 12.7); [i–vi] [1]–306

Contents [i] halftitle [ii] imprint [iii] titlepage [iv] blank [v] contents [vi] blank [1]–306 text, on 306: END OF VOL II. / [short rule] / PRINTED BY BALLANTYNE, HANSON AND CO. / EDINBURGH AND LONDON.

VOLUME III

Collation [A]–T⁸U⁶; 158 leaves (18.85 × 12.8); [i–vi] [1]–310

Contents [i] halftitle [ii] imprint [iii] titlepage [iv] blank [v] contents [vi] blank [1]–310 text, on 310: THE END. / [short rule] / PRINTED BY BALLANTYNE, HANSON AND CO. / EDINBURGH AND LONDON

Binding Spine, and boards at front and back, bound in blue cloth. Cream endpapers with a yellow coating on lining papers and recto of front free endpaper and verso of back free endpaper.

Front cover Two narrow yellow bands edged in red divide the front cover approximately into thirds. In the top third, stamped in red capital letters: THE NETHER WORLD. The middle third is enclosed by another pair of red lines, within the red-trimmed yellow lines described above; it bears a repeated motif of a plant (stem with leaves), in yellow edged with red, and arranged in regular diagonal rows against a red spotted background. In the bottom third, in red capital letters: GEORGE GISSING

Spine The yellow lines edged with red are extended over the spine. In the top third, in gilt: THE / NETHER / WORLD / [short rule] / VOL. I. The middle third has the same stem-and-leaves motif. The author's name is stamped in gilt in the lower third: GEORGE GISSING

Back cover Plain.

VII b

SECOND EDITION

THE / NETHER WORLD / A NOVEL / BY / GEORGE GISSING / AUTHOR OF 'DEMOS' ETC. / 'La peinture d'un fumier peut-être justifiée pourvu qu'il y pousse une belle fleur; sans cela, le fumier n'est que repoussant' / M. RENAN, *at the Académie Française*, Feb. 21, 1889 / A NEW EDITION / LONDON / SMITH, ELDER, & CO., 15 WATERLOO PLACE / 1890 / [*All rights reserved*]

Collation [A]⁴B–BB⁸CC⁴; 200 leaves (19 × 12.5); [i–v] vi [1]–392

Contents [i] halftitle: THE / NETHER WORLD [ii] blank [iii] titlepage [iv] blank [v]–vi contents [1]–392 text, on 392 imprint: PRINTED BY / SPOTTISWOODE AND CO., NEW-STREET SQUARE / LONDON

Binding Spine, and boards at front and back, covered in dark brown cloth. Endpapers with a primrose coating.

Front cover Stamped in brown at top and bottom a border consisting of two horizontal lines and a simple decorative band. At centre a circular ornament also stamped in brown.

Spine Between the borders at top and bottom, which have been carried over from the front cover, and stamped in gilt: THE / NETHER / WORLD / GEORGE / GISSING / SMITH ELDER & CO.

Back cover The two borders, carried over from the front cover, are blind-stamped. The back cover is otherwise plain.

PUBLICATION

After the death of his first wife, Gissing settled down in London to write *The Nether World*, which he started on 19 March 1888 and finished on 22 July. The *Diary* entries form a record of the progress of the book, which included 'fearful difficulties' with Chapter VI of the second volume and the going back to insert a 'new chapter' in the third. He sent the novel to Smith, Elder, learnt from his sister when he was already in Paris that he had been offered £150 for the copyright and, suddenly rich, spent the winter on the Continent, only returning to England at the beginning of March 1889, when he immediately corrected the proofs. Five hundred copies were printed and the book was published on 3 April 1889.

The second edition, textually identical to the first except for the correction of the eccentric punctuation, appeared in 1890 and from it, in the same year, reissues to be sold at 3/6, 2/6, and 2/- as described in the introduction.

Harper bought the American rights from Smith, Elder for £15 and the novel was published as part of the Franklin Square Library in 1889.

THE MANUSCRIPT

The manuscript of *The Nether World*, which is now in the Huntington Library, consists of a fair copy, consistently paginated in three volumes (vol. I, [1]–90; vol. II, 1–90; vol. III, 1–90), and bears the physical marks of its having been used by compositors. There is very little disturbance of the text, though perhaps the altered pagination at one or two points shows where the old and the new versions were brought together.

VIII a

THE EMANCIPATED

FIRST EDITION

THE EMANCIPATED / A Novel / BY / GEORGE GISSING / AUTHOR OF
'THE NETHER WORLD,' 'THYRZA,' ETC. / [publisher's stamp] / IN THREE
VOLUMES. / VOL. I. / LONDON: / RICHARD BENTLEY AND SON, /
Publishers in Ordinary to her Majesty the Queen. / 1890. / (*All rights
reserved.*)

VOLUME I

Collation $[\pi]^2 1-19^8 20^2$; 156 leaves (18.1 × 12.2); [i–iv] [1]–308

Contents [i] titlepage [ii] blank [iii] contents [iv] blank [1] flytitle: PART I. [2]
blank [3]–308 text, on 308: END OF VOL. I. / [short rule] / PRINTED BY WILLIAM
CLOWES AND SONS, LIMITED / LONDON AND BECCLES. G., C. & CO.

VOLUME II

Collation $[\pi]^2 21-39^8 40^2$; 156 leaves (18.1 × 12.3); [i–iv] [1]–174 [175–7] 178–306
[307–8]

Contents [i] titlepage [ii] blank [iii] contents [iv] blank [1] flytitle: PART I. /
(*Continued*) [2] blank [3]–174 text [175] flytitle: PART II. [176] blank [177]–306
text, on 306: END OF VOL. II. / [short rule] / PRINTED BY WILLIAM CLOWES AND
SONS, LIMITED, / LONDON AND BECCLES. G., C. & CO. [307–8] blank

VOLUME III

Collation $[\pi]^2 41-59^8 60^2$; 156 leaves (18.0 × 12.2); [i–viii].[1]–308

Contents [i] titlepage [ii] blank [iii] contents [iv] blank [1] flytitle: PART II. /
(*Continued*). [2] blank [3]–308 text, on 308: THE END. / [short rule] / PRINTED
BY WILLIAM CLOWES AND SONS, LIMITED, / LONDON AND BECCLES, G., C. & CO.

Binding Spine bound in dark brown cloth, extending 2.5 cms on to front and
back covers. The rest of the boards at front and back covered with light brown
patterned paper. The cream endpapers have a diagonal green pattern of crosses
creating diamond-shaped spaces within which, alternately, are the publisher's
monogram and the publisher's emblem and motto.

Front cover Plain patterned paper as described above.

Spine Stamped in gilt: THE / EMANCIPATED / [short rule] / GEORGE / GISSING / VOL. I / BENTLEY

Back cover Plain patterned paper as described above.

VIII b

SECOND EDITION

THE EMANCIPATED / *A NOVEL* / BY / GEORGE GISSING / AUTHOR OF 'THE ODD WOMEN,' 'NEW GRUB STREET,' ETC. / [publisher's stamp] / LONDON / LAWRENCE AND BULLEN / 16, HENRIETTA STREET, W.C. / 1893

Collation [A]⁴B–FF⁸GG⁴; 232 leaves (19.0 × 12.7); [i]–viii [1]–239 [240–3] 244–456

Contents [i] halftitle: THE EMANCIPATED [ii] blank [iii] titlepage [iv] imprint: LONDON. / PRINTED BY WOODFALL & KINDER, / 70–76, LONG ACRE, W.C. [v]–viii contents [1] halftitle: PART I. [2] blank [3]–239 text, on 239: [rule] [240] blank [241] halftitle: PART II. [242] blank [243]–456 text, on 456, THE END. / [rule] / Woodfall & Kinder, Printers, 70 to 76, Long Acre, London W.C.

Binding Spine, and boards at front and back, covered in deep cherry red cloth. Cream endpapers.

Front cover At top left hand corner is stamped in gilt the publisher's stamp, identical to that on titlepage.

Spine Stamped in gilt: THE / EMANCIPATED / [rule] / GEORGE / GISSING / LAWRENCE & BULLEN

Back cover Plain. Sixteen pages of publisher's advertisements, separately numbered, are sewn in at the end of some copies.

VIII c

REISSUE OF SECOND EDITION

Textually and typographically identical to Second Edition except for title-page which reads:
THE EMANICPATED / A NOVEL / BY / GEORGE GISSING / AUTHOR OF 'THE ODD WOMEN,' 'IN THE YEAR OF JUBILEE,' ETC. / THIRD EDITION / [publisher's stamp] / LONDON / LAWRENCE AND BULLEN / 16 HENRIETTA STREET, W.C. / 1895

VIII d

COLONIAL ISSUE

THE EMANCIPATED / BY / GEORGE GISSING / [publisher's stamp] /
LONDON / GEORGE BELL & SONS / AND BOMBAY / 1895

Collation [π]⁴[A]¹B⁷C–FF⁸GG⁴; 232 leaves (18.9 × 12.3); [i–vii] [1]–239 [240–3]
244–456

Contents [i] halftitle: Bell's Indian and Colonial Library / THE EMANCIPATED
[ii] blank [iii] titlepage [iv] *Issued for circulation in India and the Colonies only*
[v]–viii contents [1] flytitle: PART I. [2] blank [3]–239 text, on 239: [short rule]
[240] blank [241] flytitle: PART II. [242] blank [243]–456 text, on 456: THE END. /
[rule] / Woodfall & Kinder, Printers, 70–6, Long Acre, London W.C.

Binding Boards at front and back covered by a streaky orange-white cloth.
Cream endpapers.

Front cover Stamped in gilt: Indian & Colonial Library / THE EMANCIPATED /
[device]

Back cover Plain. Separately paginated publisher's advertisements sewn in at
the end.

PUBLICATION

The Emancipated, at first called *The Puritan*, marked the end of Gissing's
deliberate Naturalist period and the beginning of a series of psychological
novels, which were less concerned with the effects of environment and more
concerned with the emotional and intellectual conflicts experienced by socially
alienated characters. He mentioned the book in letters both to Bertz and to
his family in February 1889 (*Bertz* 52, *Letters* 279), began to think about it
seriously when he returned to England in March (the winters of 1888–9 and
1889–90 were both spent on the Continent), and then wrote it rapidly, as the
Diary and the letters confirm, between 3 June and 13 August. He felt confident
about it, knowing that, for better or worse, he had broken new ground. Indeed
his sense that something of a problem had been solved led to his taking it
immediately, on 20 August, to Bentley, as though to compensate for Bentley's
earlier rejection of *Mrs. Grundy's Enemies*. Because Bentley had paid for but
not published *Mrs. Grundy's Enemies*, Gissing now said that he 'owed' Bentley
a book, apparently unperturbed that the earlier novel had in fact been sup-

pressed on moral grounds. By comparison, this one was eminently respectable. Two women were compared. A devout, puritanical, church-going widow met an artist in Naples, read Dante, studied Italian art, matured intellectually and returned to England for a new, emancipated, civilized, agnostic, married life, while the other who, unfettered by dogma or principle, felt 'free' to elope found herself trapped by marriage and by the hypocrisy of the man who had preached freedom to her. Gissing had taken the measure of the reading public.

On 27 September 1889 Gissing recorded in the *Diary* Bentley's terms, which were an advance of £150, with an additional payment of £50 when 850 copies had been sold, and a further £50 when a thousand had been sold. Gissing's contract with Bentley, witnessed by Morley Roberts, is in the Beinecke Library. Gissing accepted these terms and duly reported them with satisfaction to Bertz (*Bertz* 74). He was to return from Greece in March 1890 in time for publication.

The Emancipated was not a great success commercially, though Gissing continued to defend it, particularly against his sister who identified herself with the values being satirized. Three years later, when Lawrence & Bullen began their attempts to gather together Gissing's copyrights, Bentley (according to the *Diary*) reported that the novel had cost £444 and had only brought in £392. He in fact sold the copyright to Lawrence & Bullen for what he called a 'nominal payment' of twenty guineas, a fact which Gissing recorded in the *Diary* and in his recollected accounts where he made the slightly curious entry: 'Bought for me by Bullen' (*Adams*).

As it turned out Gissing was no more justified in trusting Bullen commercially than his earlier publishers, but trust him he did, correcting and revising the novel in December 1892 for a one-volume edition. He recorded in the *Diary* that he made 'many corrections' and it is in fact this second edition which constitutes the definitive text.

Bullen recorded the commercial details of the publication of the second edition in a summary apparently sent to Gissing in 1895 (*Berg*). Fifteen hundred copies had been printed.

For 326 copies of the second edition (counting as 300) Gissing
received 4/- for each copy, making £60.0.0
On 162 'export' copies he made £28.7.0
And on 905 quires sold to Bell at 10½d. £40.0.0

Making a total of £128.7.0

Bullen reported the cost of printing, paper, binding (600 copies),
the fee to Bentley, and advertising to 31.12.94 £155.0.0
He further reported that he had in hand 60 copies and the plates.

These accounts confirm that sheets of the 'third edition' were sold for both the colonial issue in Bell's Indian and Colonial Library and the American issue by Way and Williams, in Chicago, 1895, of which there is a copy in the Pforzheimer Library.

THE MANUSCRIPT

The manuscript of *The Emancipated*, now in the New York Public Library, is a fair copy, which was used in the press and which is numbered consistently throughout in three volumes: 1–79; 1–80; 1–81.

IX a

NEW GRUB STREET

FIRST EDITION

NEW GRUB STREET / A NOVEL / BY / GEORGE GISSING / AUTHOR OF / 'THE NETHER WORLD' 'DEMOS' ETC. / IN THREE VOLUMES / VOL. I. / LONDON / SMITH, ELDER & CO., 15 WATERLOO PLACE / 1891 / *All rights reserved*

VOLUME I

Collation [A]^{4}B–U^{8}X^2; 158 leaves (18.9 × 12.65); [i–viii] [1]–305 [306–8]

Contents [i–ii] blank [iii] halftitle: NEW GRUB STREET / VOL. I. [iv] blank [v] titlepage [vi] blank [vii] contents [viii] blank [1]–305 text, on 305: END OF THE FIRST VOLUME. / PRINTED BY / SPOTTISWOODE AND CO., NEW-STREET SQUARE / LONDON [306] blank [307–8] publisher's advertisement

VOLUME II

Collation [A]^{4}B–X^8; 162 leaves (19 × 12.8); [i–viii] [1]–316

Contents [i–ii] blank [iii] halftitle [iv] blank [v] titlepage [vi] blank [vii] contents [viii] blank [1]–316 text, on 316: END OF THE SECOND VOLUME. / PRINTED BY / SPOTTISWOODE AND CO., NEW-STREET SQUARE / LONDON

VOLUME III

Collation [A]^{4}B–Y^8; 172 leaves (18.9 × 12.7); [i–viii] [1]–335 [336]

Contents [i–ii] blank [iii] halftitle [iv] blank [v] titlepage [vi] blank [vii] contents [viii] blank [1]–335 text, on 335: THE END / PRINTED BY / SPOTTISWOODE AND CO., NEW-STREET SQUARE / LONDON [336] blank

Binding Spine, and boards at front and back, covered in blue-green cloth simulating rough-grained leather. Yellow coating on lining papers and recto and verso of front and back free endpapers respectively.

Front cover Stamped in black at the bottom a border of two horizontal rules and at the top a border of three, above which is a faintly floral pattern. Between the two sets of horizontal borders, stamped in gilt: NEW GRUB STREET / GEORGE GISSING

Spine The borders stamped in black are continued from the front cover. Between them, stamped in gilt: NEW / GRUB / STREET / [short rule] / VOL. III / GEORGE / GISSING Beneath the lower border, also stamped in gilt: SMITH, ELDER & CO.

Back cover Plain.

IX b

REISSUE OF FIRST EDITION

New Grub Street was reissued in 1891, the only difference between the first and second edition being the words 'SECOND EDITION' on the titlepage of the latter and the black, not gilt, lettering on the spine.

IX c

SECOND EDITION

NEW GRUB STREET / A NOVEL / BY / GEORGE GISSING / AUTHOR OF 'THE NETHER WORLD' 'DEMOS' ETC / *A NEW EDITION* / LONDON / SMITH, ELDER & CO., 15 WATERLOO PLACE / 1891 / [*All rights reserved*]

Collation [A]⁴B–GG⁸HH⁴; 240 leaves (18.7 × 12.5); [i]–vi [1]–469 [470–2]

Contents [a–b] blank [i] halftitle: NEW GRUB STREET [ii] advertisement of novels by George Gissing [iii] titlepage [iv] blank [v]–vi contents [1]–469 text, on 469: [short rule] / *Spottiswoode & Co. Printers, New-street Square, London.* [470] blank [471–2] publisher's advertisement, at foot of each page: [long double rule] / LONDON: SMITH, ELDER, & CO., 15 Waterloo Place.

Binding Spine and about 3.8 cms of left and right edges of front and back covers respectively bound in dark maroon coloured cloth. Rest of front and back boards bound also in red cloth, but of a slightly different shade. Yellow coating on lining papers and recto of front and verso of back free endpapers.

Front cover Bound in two-toned red cloth as described above. Over the seam there is a border formed by two vertical narrow lines with two rows of scallops within, all stamped in black.

Spine Two sets of gilt borders at top and bottom between which, also in gilt: NEW / GRUB / STREET / GEORGE / GISSING / SMITH ELDER & C°.

Back cover As front cover.

REISSUES OF THE SECOND EDITION

As stated above, the first single-volume edition of *New Grub Street*, dated 1891, is the true second edition, though called 'a new edition' on the titlepage. Gissing neither revised it nor corrected proof. From it were prepared reissues in Smith, Elder's standard formats, all of them in the first instance dated 1892, although each was reissued as required and kept in print until after Gissing's death, the only change from issue to issue being the date. The three reissues are of course textually and typographically identical but in price, format, prelims, and binding are different. The significant differences are as follows:

IX d

THE 3/6d. REISSUE OF THE SECOND EDITION

The binding of this issue is virtually identical to that of **IX c**, the chief difference being the reduced page size, the page measuring 17.3 × 11.4.

IX e

THE 2/6d. REISSUE OF THE SECOND EDITION (page size 17.3 × 11.4)

Bound in red cloth, the lettering and design all stamped in black.

Front cover At top and bottom a double horizontal line; between the lines a simple ornamental border. Superimposed over a horizontal rectangle: NEW GRUB STREET / BY / GEORGE GISSING / AUTHOR OF / DEMOS

Spine The borders from the front cover are continued on the spine. Between them: NEW / GRUB / STREET / BY / GEORGE / GISSING / SMITH, ELDER & CO.

Back cover Plain, except for the borders at top and bottom which are continued from the front cover.

IX f

The 2/- reissue of the second edition (page size 17.3 × 11.4) Paper on boards.

Front cover Printed onto the yellow paper is a brown rectangle filling almost the whole space; there is a half centimetre border on all edges. Within this rectangle is the picture of an interior showing a man standing by a piano and a seated woman turned away from him. Above the picture: PRICE TWO SHILLINGS / *New Grub Street* Beneath: *By George Gissing* / LONDON. SMITH. ELDER. & CO.

Spine The spine is divided into seven sections by sets of horizontal rules, each pair containing a parallel row of dots. The first, third, fourth, and fifth sections contain a simple device. In the second are the words: NEW / GRUB / STREET / [short rule] / GEORGE GISSING In the sixth: TWO / SHILLINGS In the seventh: Smith, Elder & Co. The design work is predominantly dull red and brown, the lettering black.

Back cover Printed in black and covering the whole page, a fairly elaborate advertisement for 'Dr. Rooke's English Medicines'. Unlike the other reissues, the front and back endpapers of the 2/- reissue are heavy with advertisements.

TAUCHNITZ EDITION

NEW GRUB STREET / A NOVEL / BY / GEORGE GISSING, / AUTHOR OF 'DEMOS,' ETC. / *COPYRIGHT EDITION.* / IN TWO VOLUMES. / VOL. I. / LEIPZIG / BERNHARD TAUCHNITZ / 1891.

VOLUME I

Collation [1]–21⁸; 168 leaves (15.45 × 11.05); [1]–6 [7]–334 [335–6]

Contents [1] halftitle: COLLECTION / OF / BRITISH AUTHORS / TAUCHNITZ EDITION. / VOL. 2729. / NEW GRUB STREET BY GEORGE GISSING. / IN TWO VOLUMES. / VOL. I. 2 TAUCHNITZ EDITION. / By the same Author, / DEMOS . . . . 2 vols. / [short rule] [3] titlepage [4] blank [5]–6 contents 7–334 text, on 334: END OF VOL. I. [335] [medium rule] / PRINTING OFFICE OF THE PUBLISHER. / [medium rule] [336] blank

VOLUME II

Collation [1]–21⁸; 168 leaves (15.45 × 11); [1]–6 [7]–334 [335–6]

Contents [1] halftitle [2] blank [3] titlepage [4] blank [5]–6 contents [7]–334 text, on 334: THE END. [335] [medium rule] / PRINTING OFFICE OF THE PUBLISHER. / [medium rule] [336] blank

Binding Spine, and front and back covers, of cream coloured endpapers.

Front cover A frame of thin black lines runs about 1.27 cms from all sides, with decorative scroll work at the corners. At the top centre, above the top line of frame, is printed in black: EACH VOLUME SOLD SEPARATELY. Within the frame, near the top: COLLECTION / OF / BRITISH AUTHORS / TAUCHNITZ EDITION. / [short rule] / VOL. 2729 / NEW GRUB STREET BY GEORGE GISSING. / IN TWO VOLUMES. / VOL. I. / LEIPZIG: BERNHARD TAUCHNITZ. / PARIS: C. REINWALD & CIE, 15, RUE DES SAINTS-PERES. / PARIS: THE GALIGNANI LIBRARY, 224, RUE DE RIVOLI, / AND AT NICE, 16, QUAI MASSENA. And at foot of page, below lower line of frame: *This Collection / is published with copyright for Continental circulation, but all / purchasers are earnestly requested not to introduce the volumes / into England or into any British Colony.*

Spine In black: BRITISH / AUTHORS / [short rule] / TAUCHNITZ / EDITION / [short rule] / 2729 / GISSING / [short rule] / NEW GRUB / STREET / VOL. I

Back cover Publisher's advertisement printed in black on verso of back cover: JUNE 1891. / Tauchnitz Edition. / [short rule] / Latest Volumes: / [list of volumes follows] / A complete Catalogue of the Tauchnitz Edition is attached to this work. / [long rule] / Bernhard Tauchnitz, Leipzig; / And sold by all booksellers.

PUBLICATION

Gissing wrote *New Grub Street* in the brief period between his meeting, on 24 September 1890 or thereabouts, Edith Underwood who was to become his second wife, and the end of the year when he finally left Cornwall Mansions to go to Exeter. Both from his diary and correspondence, it is clear that, as far as work was concerned, he had had a bad summer; amongst other things he recorded a number of false starts on the book which was at first called *Victor Yule*. In the *Notebook* he later stated that the novel had been written between 6 October and 6 December, which is confirmed fairly precisely by his correspondence (*Letters* 311, *Bertz* 113). Though the genesis of *New Grub Street* was no doubt deep in Gissing's past, Edith Underwood provided the catalytic force during the writing of it that Gissing seemed to need, filling the same role for both *New Grub Street* and *Born in Exile* as Helen Harrison had filled for *Workers in the Dawn* and *The Unclassed*. Once again a period of desperate indecision was followed by a spurt of hard work.

The editors of *NBL* wrote about this period of work somewhat intolerantly: 'Part of Gissing's tragedy was that he felt (and often was) unable to work without the comfort and sympathy of a woman' (*NBL* 74). Being able to work hard when you enjoy the comfort and sympathy of a woman is not a tragedy and the fact that a relationship may deteriorate does not mean that it was wrong from the start. On the evidence of the *Diary*, Korg noted that 'Edith spent frequent evenings with Gissing at 7K' and that 'they passed their hours there chatting' (*Korg* 151), implying that from Gissing's point of view the relationship was a superficial one. It is easier to assume, simply, that the period between 1 March and 1 September had been one of intense frustration, that meeting Edith Underwood immediately allowed Gissing to settle to his work, that the relationship was a frankly sexual one from the outset, that their evenings and expeditions were happy ones, and that Gissing did not ask her to go to Exeter with him to chat, but for needs of his own which *New Grub Street* itself shows he understood. In such circumstances Gissing did not think critically about what he was doing; the critical stage was in the past and somewhat impulsively he simply wrote the book that had to be written.

It never seems to have occurred to Gissing that Smith, Elder might continue to grumble about the moral tone of his novels in part justification of the low offers they made for the copyright. At all events they made an offer and Gissing recorded the fact in his diary. On 7 January 1891 he wrote: 'In evening came Edith, &, by the 8.30 post at last a letter from Smith & Elder. They think *New Grub Street* clever and original, but fear it is too gloomy. Offer £150. I wrote at once accepting (ahem!) & asking them to add the £10 they offered for *Thyrza*. Heaven be thankit!' The book went to press almost immediately. Gissing corrected proofs in February and March and the novel was published on 7 April.

For some of the novels published by Smith, Elder, Gissing revised and shortened the text for publication in a single volume. In the case of *New Grub Street* he did not do so, since the book was a commercial success. Within a month the first edition was reissued and in October a single-volume edition, the true second edition, appeared. In 1892, Smith, Elder's normal reprints at 2/6 and 2/- were prepared from the same plates, all three editions (at 6/-, 2/6, and 2/-) being kept in print until after Gissing's death. All in all, the firm must have done rather well from the book – well enough for them to refuse to release the copyright for a proposed collected edition.

Because Gissing did not revise the book for Smith, Elder, his revision of it for the translation into French by Gabrielle Fleury is of considerable interest. There is abundant evidence to show that Gissing resisted the three-volume form and that he welcomed the opportunity to revise and shorten his novels not only for Smith, Elder but also for Lawrence & Bullen. The revision for the French translation is in fact on a par with the revision of his early work, in that he removed material that had been mere padding in the first edition, so that it is the French translation that in a strict sense constitutes the definitive text. It would be a logical, and extremely useful move, to have this published in English.

In his correspondence with Gabrielle Fleury, however, Gissing not only states that he cut the book to permit publication in a magazine but also gives her considerable freedom. 'Restore *anything* you like, sweet,' he says at one point (*Fleury* 111). One is therefore left with an interesting and so far unstudied textual enigma. Perhaps the French text is not entirely trustworthy. On the other hand, Gissing clearly agreed with those critics who had suggested that the elimination of superfluous dialogue would improve the book. The revised version appeared in *Le Journal des Débats* between 23 February and 3 June 1911 with the title *La Rue des Meurt-la-Faim* and in book form the following year.

It is interesting to note in passing that *New Grub Street* did not appear in North America during Gissing's lifetime.

THE MANUSCRIPT

The manuscript of *New Grub Street*, now in the Berg Collection, is a fair copy, paginated consistently in three volumes ([1]–70, [1]–70, [1]–71), and of very slight textual or critical interest. The label of a brown paper parcel which has been preserved with the MS shows that Gissing sent it to his sister Ellen from Exeter for safekeeping.

X a

DENZIL QUARRIER

FIRST EDITION

DENZIL QUARRIER / *A Novel* / BY / GEORGE GISSING / AUTHOR OF / 'New Grub Street,' 'The Nether World,' 'Thyrza,' &c. / LONDON / LAWRENCE & BULLEN / 169 NEW BOND STREET, W. / 1892

Collation [A]²B–Y⁸z³; 173 leaves (18.8.×12.35); [i–iv] [1]–341 [342]

Contents [i] halftitle: DENZIL QUARRIER [ii] blank [iii] titlepage [iv] blank [1]–341 text, on 341: THE END. / [medium rule] / PRINTED BY HENDERSON & SPALDING, LIMITED, MARYLEBONE LANE, W. [342] blank

Binding Spine, and boards at front and back, covered in green morocco cloth. Dark bluish-green coating on lining papers and recto of front free endpaper and verso of back free endpaper.

Front cover Plain except for publisher's stamp blind-stamped in middle of cover.

Spine Stamped in gilt: DENZIL / QUARRIER / [rule] / GEORGE / GISSING / LAWRENCE & BULLEN

Back cover Plain.

Variant binding As above, but in brown cloth.

X b

AMERICAN EDITION

DENZIL QUARRIER / BY / GEORGE GISSING / AUTHOR OF 'DEMOS,' ETC. / New York / MACMILLAN AND CO. / AND LONDON / 1892 / *All rights reserved˜*

Collation [1–20]⁸; 160 leaves (18.85 × 12.6); [i–iv] [1]–308 [309–16]

Contents [i] halftitle: DENZIL QUARRIER [ii] publisher's monogram [iii] titlepage [iv] copyright and imprint: COPYRIGHT, 1891, / BY / MACMILLAN & CO. / ROBERT DRUMMOND, ELECTROTYPER AND PRINTER, NEW YORK. [1]–308 text [309–16] publisher's advertisements

Binding Spine, and boards at front and back, covered in mustard yellow coloured cloth, with lettering and design work stamped in red. Cream endpapers.

Front cover A narrow red line runs vertically about 3.8 cms away from left edge. Running alongside, on its left side, is a series of seven linked wreaths, the middle wreath enclosing a circle within which is the publisher's monogram. The three wreaths above and below this each enclose an opened book. About the middle of the right half of the cover is: DENZIL / QUARRIER / BY / GEORGE / GISSING

Spine At the top is a wreath enclosing an opened book. A little below: DENZIL / QUARRIER / [device] / GEORGE / GISSING At the bottom, another wreath enclosing the publisher's stamp. Between the outer and inner circles: THE MACMILLAN COMPANY

Back cover Plain.

PUBLICATION

With *Denzil Quarrier* Gissing began his relationship with Lawrence & Bullen, which is discussed briefly in the introduction. A.H. Bullen seems to have made the first approach, for on 18 October 1891 Gissing told Bertz about the offer the firm had made. 'The new publisher, Lawrence & Bullen, who publish Roberts' new books, have written to ask me for a novel in one volume. They offer me one shilling on every 6 shilling volume sold, and, what is better, will pay £100 on account, when they publish. These terms are very liberal indeed. Accordingly, I have got to work, and am writing a book called *The Radical Candidate*' (*Bertz* 137). The *Diary* shows that he had probably received the letter from Lawrence & Bullen on 26 September 1891. The contract stipulating the terms mentioned above is dated 26 November 1891.

The novel was written very rapidly between 7 October and 12 November (if the dates in the *Notebook* are to be trusted), was sent to Lawrence & Bullen immediately, and was published on 5 February 1892.

Though he was temporarily irritated by the request that the title should be changed, it was natural for Gissing to be excited by the publication of a book for which he received an advance against royalties and he wrote enthusiastically to Bertz about the business arrangements. 'Lawrence and Bullen have done very well with the business arrangements concerning *DQ*. It is to be pub by Macmillan in New York at 1 dollar; in Australia; and by Heinemann and Balestier on the Continent. The latter have given 25 guineas. Of all foreign profits (after the £105 is repaid) I am to receive half' (*Bertz* 144–5). The novel did not do at all well, however, as the accounts in *Adams* indicate. Lawrence & Bullen's royalty report dated 31 February 1894, which indicates that the agreed terms had been that Gissing should receive 1/- for each copy of the 6/- edition sold and half profits on colonial and continental sales, lists the following items under income:

[i]   royalties on 728 copies of the 6/- edition counting as 640   32. 0.0
[ii] half profit on 250 copies to Australia at $1/10\frac{1}{2}$ 7.10.0
[iii] on 50 damaged copies sold to Samson Low   16.8
[iv] half profits on 1200 sold in quires to George Bell at $10\frac{1}{2}$ for
      a Colonial Edition   9. 7.6
[v]   half profit on Continental sale   13. 2.6
[vi] on American sales, from accounts dated 30 June 1893, 94
      and 95   8. 6.5

According to this report Gissing had received at that point his advance of £100 and two payments of 13.2.6. and 6.11.9. representing Continental and American sales. Lawrence & Bullen had in hand 194 copies bound, 500 quires on thin paper and 50 quires on thick paper, and the stereotype moulds.

Gissing was perhaps more impressed by Bullen's interest in the classics than by his business acumen.

THE MANUSCRIPT

The manuscript of *Denzil Quarrier*, which is now in the Huntington Library and is a fair copy for print-shop use with the original title deleted on page 1, would appear to be of little textual or critical significance since it corresponds except in minor detail to the first edition.

XI a

BORN IN EXILE

FIRST EDITION

BORN IN EXILE / A NOVEL / BY / GEORGE GISSING / AUTHOR OF / 'NEW GRUB STREET,' 'DENZIL QUARRIER,' ETC. / *IN THREE VOLUMES* / VOL. I / LONDON AND EDINBURGH / ADAM AND CHARLES BLACK / 1892

VOLUME I

Collation [1]⁸2–18⁸; 144 leaves (20 × 13.6); [1–6] 7–166 [167–8] 169–288

Contents [1] halftitle [2] blank [3] titlepage [4] imprint: MORRISON AND GIBB, PRINTERS, EDINBURGH. [5] PART THE FIRST [6] blank 7–166 text [167] PART THE SECOND [168] blank 169–288 text, on 288: END OF VOL. I / MORRISON AND GIBB, PRINTERS, EDINBURGH

VOLUME II

Collation [1]–17⁸; 136 leaves (19.8 × 13.7); [1–6] 7–159 [160–2] 163–271 [272]

Contents [1] halftitle: BORN IN EXILE / VOL. II [2] blank [3] titlepage [4] imprint [5] PART THE THIRD [6] blank 7–159 text [160] blank [161] PART THE FOURTH [162] blank 163–271 text, on 271: END OF VOL. II / MORRISON AND GIBB, PRINTERS, EDINBURGH [272] blank

VOLUME III

Collation [1]–17⁸; 136 leaves (19.65 × 13.7); [1–6] 7–107 [108–10] 111–270 [271–2]

Contents [1] halftitle [2] blank [3] titlepage [4] imprint [5] PART THE FIFTH [6] blank 7–107 text [108] blank [109] PART THE SIXTH [110] blank 111–270 text, on 270; THE END. / MORRISON AND GIBB, PRINTERS, EDINBURGH. [271–2] advertisements

Binding Spine, and boards at front and back, covered in purplish-brown cloth. Endpapers have yellow background formed by close fine yellow lines running vertically. Superimposed on this is a floral motif of sprigs of plants, with leaves and flowers, in white and outlined in yellow, running in more or less horizontal rows.

Front cover Plain except for a narrow black border running about 1 cm from all edges.

Spine At the top in gilt: BORN / IN / EXILE / [short rule] / G. GISSING

Back cover Identical to front cover.
The novel was reissued in 1893 in blue cloth, in 1896 as a yellow back.

PUBLICATION

The external evidence strongly suggests that *Born in Exile* was written in two parts, the first part before the death of his first wife, the second immediately after his marriage to his second wife. (It must be stated in fairness that there are critics who, though they appear not to have examined the manuscript, hold a contrary opinion.)

The *Diary* entries which indicate that Gissing was writing *Born in Exile* in January 1888 suggest that he had begun it late in 1887. At all events he was working hard during the first week of 1888 and on 7 January wrote in the *Diary*: 'Finished, thank heaven, the Chapter of Peak's antecedents.' He mentioned that this was chapter VII, which corresponds to the novel as we now have it. On 12 January the *Diary* entry is as follows: 'Began to write at 4.30, & went on till 9.30, with effort. Did nearly 5 pages, however, bringing me to 75 of Vol. I.' The manuscript of volume I consists of 79 pages but the disturbance of the pagination indicates that 4 pages were introduced at a later stage. On 16 January he entered in the *Diary* that he had finished volume I and on 7 February that he had begun a new novel, which he tentatively called *Marian Dane*. Later in February he received news of his wife's death and returned to London from Eastbourne. Not much is known about Gissing's personal habits as a writer, but this was neither the first nor the last time that he had put down part of a novel only to pick it up at a later date. There remains a critical problem. Volume I of *Born in Exile* seems juvenile not only when compared with volumes II and III, but also in comparison with early novels like *Demos* and *Thyrza*. Possibly the sections on 'Peake' and his antecedents, which critics like Korg relate so firmly to Gissing's student days, were written earlier than 1888, though this is a critical speculation that requires an extended discussion perhaps inappropriate in a bibliography.

Gissing returned to the writing of *Born in Exile* in the spring of 1891, immediately after his marriage to Edith Underwood on 25 February. The *Diary* entry for 2 March states: 'Sat down in my den at the top of the house, & worked at plan of new book.' Further entries mark the progress of the book.

4 March 'worked at novel in the morning: think it will be called *Raymond Peak*'
6 May 'finishing Vol. I.'
15 June 'finishing Vol. II.'
17 July 'finishing *Godwin Peak*.'

The firmness of these entries, the details of which are confirmed in Gissing's correspondence with Bertz, has made critics take them literally. In fact, though, the status of the *Diary* has yet to be determined. Was it an *aide mémoire* or was it intended for his wives?

From the *Diary* one knows that on 20 July Gissing sent *Born in Exile* to Smith and Elder with a request for £250 for the English and the American rights. After a delay which Gissing found doubly irritating in that Payn, the reader, kept it a long time and then made suggestions for revision which were unacceptable to Gissing, or at first seemed so, he handed the book over to an agent, A.P. Watt, who had refusals in fairly rapid succession from at least three publishers: Chatto and Windus, Longman's, and Bentley. Not until the end of December did Gissing learn that the book had been accepted by A. and C. Black. On 15 January 1892 he told Bertz about it: 'You will be glad to hear that Watt has at last sold *Godwin Peak*. Mess. A and C Black (very solid publishers who are just beginning to extend their business) have bought the British rights for £150. Out of this I have to pay Watt 10 per cent, so that my hope of getting *more* through him is frustrated. The book will not be pub[lished] before next October. Before then, I shall revise it' (*Bertz* 142). As far as one can judge, the manuscript had been out of Gissing's hands continuously from 20 July 1891 to 12 January 1892.

Gissing had in fact written to A. and C. Black on 8 January 1892 to inform them that he would need to revise the novel and the revision was done between 12 January, when the manuscript was returned to him and 6 February, when he sent it back to Edinburgh. The details of this revision can be followed fairly closely in the manuscript, not just because of the disruption which resulted in the renumbering of pages but also because Gissing changed the names of some of his characters as he worked. The parts of the novel in which the two main women characters, Sidwell Warricombe and Marcella Moxey, appear, were largely rewritten. A final revision occurred when the novel was in proof. The *Diary* entry for 29 March 1892 reads as follows: 'On receiving final proofs of *Born in Exile*, find that Vol III runs only to 249 pp. This is too short. Resolved to insert a chapter before the last, & wrote to publishers saying this should be sent.' Neither the major revision nor the addition of the penultimate chapter has so far been studied in any detail.

Born in Exile was published in three volumes on 29 April 1892, 500 copies being prepared in this form according to *NBL*. A. and C. Black issued the novel in single volume form at least twice. In 1893 a cheaper single volume impression was published in both a maroon and a blue cloth binding: several copies dated 1894 have also been noted. Later a 2/- 'yellowback' was issued, the copy inspected being dated 1896. In the same year, Lawrence & Bullen purchased the British rights for £110.10 but did not publish the novel, which remained out of print until 1910. It is interesting to note Clara Collet's letter to Pinker dated 10 February 1907 in which she advised him to negotiate with Mr Bullen over the rights to Gissing's work, 'except for *Born in Exile* of which the rights are mine entirely and which Mr. Bullen never published' (*Berg*). Much later, on 9 September 1920, Alfred Gissing told Pinker that the copyright of nine books had 'gone' to Clara Collet, one of them being *Born in Exile* (*Berg*). (The others were *The Unclassed, The Emancipated, Denzil Quarrier, In the Year of Jubilee, Eve's Ransom, The Whirlpool, The Odd Women*, and *Human Odds and Ends*.)

THE MANUSCRIPT

The manuscript of *Born in Exile*, which is in the Huntington Library, is a fair copy that was used in the press. The three volumes, all of which have been divided for the compositor and indeed carry the compositors' names, have a continuous though greatly corrected pagination: Volume I, [1]–79; Volume II, [1]–76; and Volume III, [1]–69 [1]–7 70–74. The separately paged chapter in Volume III has also been referred to under *Publication*. Apart from this, the chief feature of the manuscript is the considerable disturbance of the pagination. A break or a disturbance in the sequence of page numbers could, of course, result from a mere error in counting. In the case of *Born in Exile*, however, the pagination can be related to the process of revision with a fair degree of certainty. Though further study seems necessary, its physical features make this one of the more interesting of Gissing manuscripts.

XII a

THE ODD WOMEN

FIRST EDITION

THE ODD WOMEN / BY / GEORGE GISSING / Author of 'New Grub Street,' 'Demos,' &c. / IN THREE VOLUMES. / [publisher's stamp] VOL. I. / LONDON / LAWRENCE & BULLEN / 16 HENRIETTA STREET, COVENT GARDEN, W.C. / 1893

VOLUME I

Collation [A]^{4}B–T^{8}U^4[v]^1; 153 leaves (18.55 × 12.2); [i–viii] [1]–296 [297–8]

Contents [i–ii] blank [iii] halftitle: THE ODD WOMEN / VOL. I. [iv] blank [v] titlepage [vi] imprint: LONDON: / HENDERSON AND SPALDING, LIMITED, / MARYLEBONE LANE, W. [vii] contents [viii] blank [1]–296 text, on 296; END OF VOL. I. [297–8] blank

VOLUME II

Collation [A]^{4}B–x^{8}y^6; 170 leaves (18.4 × 12.1); [i–viii] [1]–330 [331–2]

Contents [i–ii] blank [iii] halftitle [iv] blank [v] titlepage [vi] imprint [vii] contents [viii] blank [1]–330 text, on 330: END OF VOL. II. [331–2] blank

VOLUME III

Collation [A]^{4}B–x^{8}y^4; 168 leaves (18.5 × 12.1); [i–viii] [1]–325 [326–8]

Contents [i–ii] blank [iii] halftitle [iv] blank [v] titlepage [vi] imprint [vii] contents [viii] blank [1]–325 text, on 325: THE END. [326–8] blank

Binding Spine, and boards at front and back, covered in maroon coarse morocco cloth. The endpapers are patterned, with a background of fine yellowish-green diagonal lines on white. Over this is a floral pattern with star-shaped flowers and sprigs of leaves in green and white.

Front cover About 0.65 cms from top and bottom edges run two borders, blind-stamped, each formed by one broader line and a group of three narrower lines. The border at the bottom is a little broader than the one at the top.

Spine The borders are extended over the spine. At the top, beneath the top border, in gold: THE / ODD / WOMEN / [rule] / GEORGE / GISSING / VOL. I. At the bottom, in the border between the group of lines and the thicker single line, in gold: LAWRENCE & BULLEN

Back cover Top and bottom lined borders are extended over back cover.

XII b

SECOND EDITION

THE ODD WOMEN / BY / GEORGE GISSING / AUTHOR OF 'NEW GRUB STREET,' ETC. / NEW EDITION / [publisher's stamp] / LA WRENCE & BULLEN / 16 HENRIETTA STREET, COVENT GARDEN, W.C. / 1894

Collation $[\pi]^4$1–28^8; 228 leaves (19×13); [i–vi] vii–viii [1]–446 [447–8]

Contents [i–ii] blank [iii] halftitle: THE ODD WOMEN [iv] blank [v] titlepage [vi] blank vii–viii contents [1]–446 text, on 446: THE END / [rule] / PRINTED BY HENDERSON & SPALDING, LTD., FROM AMERICAN PLATES. [447–8] blank 16 separately numbered pages of publisher's advertisements have been sewn into most copies.

Binding Spine, and boards at front and back, covered with a maroon cloth with a vertical ribbing. Dark green endpapers.

Front cover Plain.

Spine Stamped in gilt and with title and publisher's name enclosed in a simple rectangle: THE / ODD / WOMEN / GEORGE / GISSING / LAWRENCE & BULLEN

Back cover Plain.

XII c

REISSUE OF SECOND EDITION

THE ODD WOMEN / BY / GEORGE GISSING / NEW AND CHEAPER EDITION / LONDON / A.H. BULLEN / 47 GREAT RUSSELL STREET / 1905

Collation $[\pi]^4$[1]–28^8; 228 leaves (18.4×12.2); [i]–viii 1–446 [447–8]

Contents [i–ii] blank [iii] halftitle: THE ODD WOMEN [iv] blank [v] titlepage [vi] blank vii–viii contents 1–446 text, on 446: THE END / UNWIN BROTHERS, LIMITED, PRINTERS, WOKING AND LONDON. [447–8] publisher's advertisement, at foot of [448]: [short rule] / A.H. BULLEN, 47 GREAT RUSSELL ST., LONDON, W.C.

Binding Spine, and boards at front and back, covered in medium green coloured cloth. Cream endpapers.

Front cover About 2.55 cms from top edge is stamped in black: THE ODD WOMEN

Spine At the top is stamped in black: THE / ODD / WOMEN / GEORGE / GISSING.

Back cover Plain.

There are at least two versions of this reissue. The first is identical to the second, described above, except that the date is 1901 and the binding is in the same maroon cloth as the original second edition.

PUBLICATION

Gissing probably began to think about the novel that was to become *The Odd Women* during the spring of 1892. On 16 February 1892 he wrote to Bertz about a number of books and said that he had in mind a novel which 'will present those people who, congenitally incapable of true education, have yet been taught to consider themselves too good for manual, or any humble, work. As yet I have chiefly dealt with types expressing the struggle of natures endowed *above* their stations; now I turn to those who are *below* it. The story will be a study of vulgarism – the all but triumphant force of our time. Women will be the chief characters' (*Bertz* 144).

It is interesting to note that here, as elsewhere, there is a discrepancy – an understandable one – between the running entries in the *Diary* on the one hand and the terser statements of fact in the *Notebook* on the other. The *Diary* entries show that Gissing had difficulty with the novel, that it took time for him to work himself into it, that during July 1892 he made at least eight and perhaps as many as twelve false starts, and that on 30 July he 'decided to throw away all' he had written. In his later summary, however, he said he wrote *The Odd Women* in seven weeks between 18 August and 4 October 1892. From this we gather that, when Gissing states that he wrote a novel in a certain period of weeks or months, he refers, not to the total time during which he was in some sense 'working' on the book, but rather to the intense, final but much shorter period in which he produced the version of the novel actually submitted to the publisher. *The Odd Women* constitutes a minor example of this type of discrepancy or enigma. When Gissing finished the novel, however, he recorded the fact in his *Diary* on 4 October: 'finished the last chapter. I shall call the book *The Odd Women*. I have written it very quickly, but the writing has been as severe a struggle as I ever knew. Not a day without wrangling and uproar down in the kitchen; not an hour when I was really at peace in mind. A bitter struggle.' Bitter struggle or not he sent the novel off to Lawrence & Bullen the following day.

From the *Diary* one knows that Lawrence & Bullen offered a royalty of 3/- on the three-volume edition, and of 6d. on a subsequent 3/6d. edition, but with an advance of 100 guineas against royalties. Later, on 11 March 1893, he gave further details in a letter to Bertz: 'Here is an account of the arrangements for the foreign publication of *The Odd Women*. For their continental issue, Heinemann and Balestier have given 35 guineas; for their Colonial, they have purchased 1500 copies, in sheets, these sheets to be supplied by Macmillans from New York. The American issue is to be at a dollar' (*Bertz* 168). Gissing did not realize at the time that these were not really very good terms for 1892–3. In point of fact he was to receive little for the book beyond the advance on royalty, yet because of the civilized relationship that Gissing had with Lawrence & Bullen – civilized in the sense that Gissing felt he was dealing with people who understood him – he continued to be happy with the arrangement until Colles taught him that better terms could be negotiated.

Gissing corrected proof between 18 and 22 November and later rewrote the first two chapters at Bullen's request. The novel was published on 10 April 1893. Lawrence & Bullen's royalty statement, made up to the end of 1894, a report somewhat at variance with the details Gissing entered earlier in his *Diary*, states that the terms were 4/- per copy on the 3 volume edition, 1/- per copy on the 6/- edition, and half profits on colonial and continental sales. Sales to that point were given as follows:

3 vol. at 4/-	66. 4.0
563/520 1 vol.	26. 0.0
Half profits in Continental Sale	18. 7.6
Half profits of sale to Heinemann	8. 3.0
1500 at 10 pence per copy	
Half profits in American sale:	
to 30.6.93	3.12.0
to end of '94	1. 0.8
	123. 7.2

A separate note indicates that Gissing was paid:

An advance of	105. 0.0
Half profits on the continental sales	18. 7.6
An additional	26. 5.0
	149.12.6

Lawrence & Bullen had printed 750 copies of the first edition and bound 400. 60 bound copies had been given away, 8 were in stock, 1 was the office copy, and 331 had been sold. They reported 354 quire copies in stock.

XIII a

IN THE YEAR OF JUBILEE

FIRST EDITION

IN THE YEAR OF / JUBILEE / BY / GEORGE GISSING / AUTHOR OF 'THE ODD WOMEN,' 'THE EMANCIPATED,' ETC. / IN THREE VOLUMES / VOL. I / [Publisher's stamp] / LONDON / LAWRENCE AND BULLEN / 16 HENRIETTA STREET, COVENT GARDEN, W.C. / 1894

VOLUME I

Collation $[\pi]^2$A–O^{8}P^6; 120 leaves (18.6 × 12.1); [i–iv] [1]–134 [135–6] 137–236

Contents [i] halftitle: IN THE YEAR OF JUBILEE / VOL. I [ii] blank [iii] titlepage [iv] blank [1] flytitle: Part the First / MISS LORD [2] blank [3]–134 text [135] flytitle: Part the second / NATURE'S GRADUATE [136] blank 137–236 text, on 236: END OF VOL. I. / *Printed by* BALLANTYNE, HANSON & CO. / *Edinburgh and London*

VOLUME II

Collation $[\pi]^2$A–Q^{8}R^6; 136 leaves (18.55 × 12.2); [i–iv] [1]–130 [131–2] 133–266 [267–8]

Contents [i] halftitle [ii] blank [iii] titlepage [iv] blank [1] flytitle: Part the Third / INTO BONDAGE [2] blank [3]–130 yext [131] flytitle: Part the Fourth / THE VEILED FIGURE [132] blank 133–266 text, on 266: END OF VOL. II / *Printed by* BALLANTYNE, HANSON & CO. / *Edinburgh and London* [267–8] blank

VOLUME III

Collation $[\pi]^2$A–Q^{8}R^6; 136 leaves (18.5 × 12); [i–iv] [1]–155 [156–8] 159–268

Contents [i] halftitle [ii] blank [iii] titlepage [iv] blank [1] flytitle: Part the Fifth / COMPASSED ROUND [2] blank 3–155 text [156] blank [157] flytitle: Part the Sixth / A VIRTUE OF NECESSITY [158] blank 159–268 text, on 268: THE END. / *Printed by* BALLANTYNE, HANSON & CO. / *Edinburgh and London.*

Binding Spine, and boards at front and back, covered in dark blue morocco cloth. White endpapers.

Front cover Blind-stamped at the top and bottom are borders consisting of parallel lines of varying thickness.

Spine The line borders at top and bottom are extended over spine. Stamped in gilt: IN THE / YEAR / OF / JUBILEE / [rule] / GEORGE / GISSING / VOL. I / LAWRENCE & BULLEN

Back cover As front cover.

XIII b

SECOND EDITION

IN THE YEAR OF / JUBILEE / BY / GEORGE GISSING / AUTHOR OF 'THE ODD WOMEN,' 'THE EMANCIPATED,' ETC. / [publisher's stamp] / NEW EDITION / LONDON / LAWRENCE AND BULLEN / 16 HENRIETTA STREET, COVENT GARDEN, W.C. / 1895.

Collation $[\pi]^2$A–2D^{8}2E^6; 224 leaves (19.2 × 12.8); [i–iv] [1]–443 [444]

Contents [i] halftitle: IN THE YEAR OF JUBILEE [ii] blank [iii] titlepage [iv] imprint: *Printed by* BALLANTYNE, HANSON & CO. / *At the Ballantyne Press* [1]–443 text, on 443: THE END. / *Printed by* BALLANTYNE, HANSON & CO. / *Edinburgh and London* [444] blank

Binding Spine, and boards at front and back, covered in deep maroon cloth. Bluish-green coating on lining papers and recto of front free endpaper and verso of back free endpaper.

Front cover Plain.

Spine Stamped in gilt and with title and publisher's names within a simple rectangle: IN THE / YEAR / OF / JUBILEE / GEORGE / GISSING / LAWRENCE & BULLEN

Back cover Plain.

The second edition in one volume appeared in two forms, since A.H. Bullen reissued the volume described here when Lawrence and Bullen was dissolved, the only difference between the two being the spine where 'Lawrence & Bullen' is replaced by 'A.H. Bullen.' Note, however, that some copies of the second edition are dated 1894 in error. One such copy in the Berg Collection has the following inscription, dated 10 January 1895 and signed by H. Walton Lawrence: 'to Reina E Lawrence from Harry Lawrence (of Lawrence & Bullen) this first copy of Gissing's *In the Year of Jubilee* in one volume form with a unique title page, date 1894 which was printed in error.'

XIII c

AMERICAN EDITION

IN THE YEAR OF JUBILEE / *A NOVEL* / BY / GEORGE GISSING / AUTHOR OF / EVE'S RANSOM, THE ODD WOMEN, DENZIL QUARRIER, ETC. / [publisher's stamp] / NEW YORK / D. APPLETON AND COMPANY / 1895

Collation $[\pi]^1[1]$–$26^8[27]^1$; 210 leaves (17.5 × 11.7); [i–vi] 1–404 [405–14]

Contents [i] blank [ii] blank [iii] halftitle [iv] blank [v] titlepage [vi] copyright: COPYRIGHT, 1894, / BY GEORGE GISSING. / COPYRIGHT, 1895, / BY D. APPLETON AND COMPANY. 1–404 text, on 404: THE END. [405–12] publisher's advertisement [413–4] blank

Binding Spine, and boards at front and back, covered in green cloth. Blue coating on lining papers, and on recto of front free endpaper and verso of back free endpaper.

Front cover Stamped in gilt-edged red and enclosed within a scrolled frame: IN THE / YEAR OF / JUBILEE / GEORGE GISSING

Spine Stamped in gilt-edged red: IN THE / YEAR OF / JUBILEE / [short rule] / GISSING / [device] / APPLETONS

Back cover Plain.

PUBLICATION

Though the period during which Gissing wrote *In the Year of Jubilee* is identified in the *Notebook* as 1 January–13 April 1894, Gissing had as usual made many starts throughout the late summer and autumn, as a number of entries in the *Diary* indicate. Even when he finished it, he called it 'my interminable novel,' for he had had difficulty not only with the story itself but with its tone. He had to explain his satirical intentions to his family and, in the same vein, later wrote to Bertz: 'Of course it has a satirical significance, and I hope you will not be dissatisfied with my picture of certain detestable phases of modern life' (*Bertz* 188).

The book, originally to have been called *Miss Lord of Camberwell*, was renamed while Gissing was correcting proof. *NBL* states: 'For the work Bullen paid an advance of 100 guineas, but by 1898 Gissing had earned only £132 from the book, originally titled *Miss Lord of Camberwell* and renamed in proof when Gissing was revising it. It was Gissing's last three-decker, published in the year of the collapse of the traditional method of publishing fiction. Appleton published the American edition and George Bell took 150 sets in sheets for the

Colonies' (NBL 94–5). As a matter of fact the contract, dated 1 June 1894, specified that the book was to be published that year, that 600 copies were to be printed, that Gissing was to receive 4/6 on every copy and half the profits arising from American, continental, and colonial sales, and that the novel would afterwards be reissued in 1 volume at 6/-, Gissing to receive 1/- for each copy sold. Further, Gissing was to receive 50 guineas on receipt of the MS and 50 guineas on the day of publication.

In both the Notebook and in Adams Gissing stated that he received an advance of £105. According to Adams, subsequent receipts were 1895 £20.3.0; 1896 £2.18.0; 1897 £3.12.0; to June 1898 7/-. The dates are significant since correspondence in the Lilly Library in Bloomington states that Lawrence & Bullen transferred the copyright to Appleton Century on 13 April 1895 for a payment of £50. This adds piquancy to later developments. When A.C. Gissing wrote to Appleton Century in 1926 about the possibility of a collected edition, he was told in a letter dated 18 August 1926 that the plates had been sold to Burt in 1905, information which of course is consistent with Burt's reissue of that date. The following week Appleton Century offered to sell the copyright to A.C. Gissing for $300. A.H. Bullen's decision to reissue the surplus stock of the Lawrence & Bullen edition of 1894 with his own name on the spine and titlepage is thus, to say the least, something of a deviation from the fair dealing for which Gissing had prized his friendship.

THE MANUSCRIPT

The manuscript of In the Year of Jubilee, now in the Huntington, is of considerable interest. It is a fair copy prepared for the press, paginated consistently throughout (volume I [1]–67; volume II 68–139; and volume III 140–207), and with the usual physical evidence of its having been used by compositors. The title is Nancy Lord of Camberwell, but pencilled on the first page in a different hand is the notation: '600 copies Title to be simply Miss Lord.'

The manuscript, with a fair number of corrections and deletions, does not correspond precisely to the text of the first edition.

XIV a

EVE'S RANSOM

FIRST EDITION

EVE'S RANSOM / BY / GEORGE GISSING / AUTHOR OF / 'THE ODD WOMEN,' 'THE EMANCIPATED,' 'IN THE / YEAR OF JUBILEE,' ETC. ETC. / [publisher's stamp] / LONDON / LAWRENCE & BULLEN / 16 HENRIETTA STREET, COVENT GARDEN, W.C. / 1895

Collation $[\pi]^2[1]-23^824^6$; 192 leaves (19.0 × 12.7); [i–iv] 1–379 [380] [1]–16

Contents [i] halftitle: EVE'S RANSOM [ii] blank [iii] titlepage [iv] blank 1–379 text, on 379: THE END. / *Printed from American Plates* / BALLANTYNE, HANSON & CO. / *London & Edinburgh* [380] blank [1]–16 publisher's advertisement bound in

Binding Spine, and boards at front and back, bound in deep maroon cloth.

Front cover Plain.

Spine With the title and the name of the publisher contained within simple frames and all stamped in gilt: EVE'S / RANSOM / GEORGE / GISSING / LAWRENCE & BULLEN

Back cover Plain.

XIV b

REISSUE OF FIRST EDITION

The reissue of the first edition in 1895 is identical to the first edition except for the addition of the words '*SECOND EDITION*' on the titlepage. The copies of this reissue that were inspected did not contain the advertisements that were bound into the first edition.

XIV b

FIRST AMERICAN EDITION

EVE'S RANSOM / *A NOVEL* / BY / GEORGE GISSING / AUTHOR OF DENZIL QUARRIER, THE ODD WOMEN, / IN THE YEAR OF JUBILEE, ETC. / [publisher's stamp] / NEW YORK / D. APPLETON AND COMPANY / 1895

Collation $[\pi]^1[1]-24^8[25]^1$; 194 leaves (17.9 × 12.0); [i–iv] 1–379 [380–4]

Contents [i–ii] blank [iii] titlepage [iv] copyright: COPYRIGHT, 1895, / BY D. APPLETON AND COMPANY. 1–379 text, on 379: THE END. [380–2] publisher's advertisement [383–4] blank

Binding Spine, and boards at front and back, covered in green cloth. Blue coating on lining papers and on recto of front free endpaper and verso of back free endpaper.

Front cover At the top left and enclosed within a device is stamped in gilt-edged red: EVE'S / RANSOM / GEORGE GISSING

Spine Stamped in gilt-edged red: EVE'S / RANSOM / [short rule] / GISSING / [device] / APPLETONS

Back cover Plain.

PUBLICATION

Eve's Ransom was a commissioned novel written against the grain, though H.G. Wells was to call it 'the best and the least appreciated of his novels.' To Clement Shorter's request that he should write a story for serialization in the *Illustrated London News*, Gissing wrote back from Brixton on 25 January 1894: 'I am obliged by your letter, in which you state particulars concerning the serial story I am to write for the *Illustrated London News*.

This story, of 60,000 words or so, I hope to be able to let you have, complete, not later than the beginning of July next. I am glad to know that you may possibly use it this year.

I may mention that the scene will be, partly in the Black Country, partly in London. The characters will be chiefly educated people' (*Huntington*). Yet it was easier to promise the book than to write it. Here is an example of the mere toil to which Wells referred in his preface to *Veranilda*. Late in April Gissing told his brother that he was 'struggling with rather over-worn mind to get to Shorter's story. Nothing written yet' (*Berg*). Eventually, having moved to Clevedon, he wrote the book in a burst of energy in twenty-five days, between 4 and 29 June, dates confirmed by both the *Diary* and the *Notebook*. He had met his deadline, was paid £150 by Shorter and corrected the proofs in July, though the serial did not in fact appear until the following year when it ran in the *Illustrated London News* from 5 January to 30 March 1895.

Adams shows that Gissing's receipts in the book publication of *Eve's Ransom* were an advance of £52.10, followed by payments of £23.2.1 in June 1895; £3.50 in December 1895; 10/- in 1896; £2.14 in 1897; and £1.6 in the first part of 1898. He also received £9 for French translation rights. *NBL* (p 101) gives the impression that Lawrence & Bullen behaved generously over *Eve's Ransom*. The contrary appears to be the case. No doubt Gissing was relieved to receive the advance on royalties in addition to the payment for the serial, but since the book was at least modestly successful (the first printing of 1000 copies was sold quickly) Gissing could perhaps have expected to have done better from a 20 per cent royalty on a book selling at 6/-. Excluding the payment for translation rights, he seems to have received a total of just over £83.0.0 for the book, so that one is forced to the conclusion that it was not Bullen's actual practice but his manner which Gissing liked. Colles had in fact urged

Gissing to find a new publisher for *Eve's Ransom* but Gissing had replied: 'it would be too bad to go elsewhere with it after their standing by me through the evil days.'

Because of the recently enacted American copyright law, *Eve's Ransom* was first printed and published in the States, the English first edition being a reissue from the American plates. Publication was almost simultaneous. Of the English issue, a second impression was made in 1895 (called SECOND EDITION on the titlepage) and later, in 1901, A.H. Bullen attempted to dispose of the old stock. Two versions are known. One is dated 1901, has a new titlepage which specifies 'new edition' and 'A.H. Bullen' as publisher, and has 'A.H. Bullen' not 'Lawrence & Bullen' on the spine. The other is dated 1895, does not have a new titlepage, but does have 'A.H. Bullen' not 'Lawrence & Bullen' on the spine.

Though there are a few minor textual differences between the serial and the first edition, they appear to have been editorial. 'What the devil does this mean,' for example, is changed to 'What does this mean.' The other changes are of this unimportant kind and it is most unlikely that Gissing himself had any hand in the preparation of the first edition text, in which case the copy text for this novel would, strictly speaking, be that of the serial for which he corrected proof. Nor had Gissing any hand in the translation into French by Georges Art which appeared in the *Revue de Paris* between 1 April and 15 May 1898 and, as *La Rançon d'Eve*, was published in book form by Calmann-Levy in the same year.

THE MANUSCRIPT

The manuscript of *Eve's Ransom*, now in the Huntington, is a fair copy with very few corrections or emendations but with the clear physical evidence of its having been used by compositors.

XV a

THE PAYING GUEST

FIRST EDITION

THE PAYING GUEST / BY / GEORGE GISSING / *Author of 'In the Year of Jubilee,' 'The Odd / Women,' etc.* / [short rule] / CASSELL AND COMPANY, LIMITED / *LONDON, PARIS & MELBOURNE* / 1895 / ALL RIGHTS RESERVED

Collation [A]–J^8[K]^2; 82 leaves (16.0×8.9); [1]–[4] 5–158 [159–64]

Contents [1] title of series: CASSELL'S POCKET LIBRARY / *Edited by* / MAX PEM-
PERTON [2] publisher's advertisement [3] titlepage [4] publisher's stamp 5–[159]
text, on [159]: [short rule] / Printed by Cassell & Co., Ltd., La Belle Sauvage,
London, E.C. [160] blank [161–4] publisher's advertisement, at foot of [164]:
Cassell & Company, Limited, Ludgate Hill, London.

Binding Spine, and boards at front and back, covered in mustard-yellow calico.
White endpapers.

Front cover On the left of the cover, stamped in red, is a vertical border consisting of the branches of a tree or plant at the roots of which, enclosed in a
small square, is the price: 1s/4d. On the right, also stamped in red: THE PAYING /
GUEST / GEORGE / GISSING / CASSELL'S / POCKET LIBRARY / EDITED BY / MAX
PEMPERTON

Spine Stamped in red: THE / PAYING / GUEST / GEORGE GISSING / CASSELL &
COMPY. / LMTD.

Back cover A small device stamped in red at centre.

XV b

The first edition was also published in fawn wrappers.

XV c

AMERICAN EDITION

THE / PAYING GUEST / BY / GEORGE GISSING / [small scroll work design]
/ NEW YORK / DODD, MEAD & COMPANY / 1895

Collation 96 leaves (15.65×9.2); [1–6] 7–191 [192]

Contents [1–2] blank [3] halftitle: THE PAYING GUEST [4] blank [5] titlepage [6]
imprint: COPYRIGHT, 1895, BY / DODD, MEAD & COMPANY / THE GUARANTEE
PRESS / NEW YORK 7–191 text [192] blank

Binding Spine, and boards at front and back, covered in mustard-yellow cloth.
Beige endpapers.

Front cover At the top, printed in black, the design of an English £5 banknote,
the date of which is also that of the novel. Superimposed on it is: THE PAYING
GUEST. At the bottom left corner is stamped in red: GEORGE GISSING

Spine Stamped in red: THE / PAYING / GUEST / [a small device] / GISSING / DODD, MEAD / & COMPANY

Back cover Plain.

PUBLICATION

Little is known about *The Paying Guest*. It was the third of the single-volume novels that Gissing wrote virtually on commission, was regarded as a potboiler from start to finish, and was soon forgotten. The memorandum of agreement with Cassell, which Gissing signed on 27 April 1895, stipulated a payment of £50 for the world copyright (excluding the US) of a 25,000-word book to be delivered by 31 October 1895.

Gissing must have written it very much less than a month after completing *Eve's Ransom*, since the start of it he recorded in the *Diary*: 'Invitation from Shorter to be his guest at the dinner of Omar Khayyam Club at Burford Bridge Hotel, on Saturday of next week. George Meredith to be there – accepted. Made a new vigorous start; story to be called *The Paying Guest*.' That was on 2 July 1895. The novel was finished within the month and published in the autumn.

The independent contract with Dodd, Mead for the American edition was dated 3 January 1896 and specified a 10 per cent royalty on all copies sold, though there is no evidence that Gissing received income from the book. Actually, there is no evidence that he gave the book a further thought. He quickly moved on to another potboiler. From *Adams* we know that for *The Paying Guest* Gissing was paid £50 by Cassell and an advance against a 10 per cent royalty by Dodd, Mead. There is no evidence that Gissing expected a further return from the English edition.

XVI a

SLEEPING FIRES

FIRST EDITION

George Gissing [facsimile signature] / SLEEPING FIRES / BY / *GEORGE GISSING* / AUTHOR OF / 'THE ODD WOMEN,' 'EVE'S RANSOM,' &c. / [leaf-shaped design] / LONDON / T. FISHER UNWIN / 1895

Collation [A]–P⁸; 120 leaves (17.05×9.3); [1]–[6] 7–229 [230] [231–40]

Contents [1] advertisements of The Autonym Library [2] advertisement of The Pseudonym Library [3] halftitle: Autonym Library [on a scroll-shaped device] / SLEEPING FIRES / [device] [4] blank [5] titlepage [6] copyright statement: COPYRIGHT BY T. FISHER UNWIN / *for Great Britain* / and the *United States of America* 7–[230] text, on [230]: THE END. / UNWIN BROTHERS, CHILWORTH AND LONDON. [231–40] publisher's advertisement: Catalogue of books published by Mr. T. Fisher Unwin

Binding Spine, and boards at front and back, covered in buff cloth.

Front cover 1.25 cms from top and bottom edges are borders formed by five horizontal rows of blue circles of graded sizes – the row of largest circles forming the side closer to the edge. On the top half of the cover is stamped in dark blue: SLEEPING / FIRES / BY GEORGE / GISSING. A little above the lower border, also in blue: AUTONYM LIBRARY

Spine The two borders are extended to the spine from the front cover. Between them, stamped in dark blue: THE / AUTONYM / LIBRARY / SLEEPING / FIRES / BY / GEORGE GISSING

Back cover The two borders run over the spine onto and over the back cover. About the middle is a leaf-shaped device, identical to that on the halftitle, but here in blue instead of black, though with same white scroll work.

XVI b

REISSUE OF THE FIRST EDITION

The first edition of *Sleeping Fires* was reissued by Fisher Unwin in 1895 in rose pink or salmon coloured wrappers. The reissue is in all respects the same as the first edition, except for the binding, which is as follows:

Front cover Printed on the wrapper: [a device] / Autonym Library / Sleeping Fires, by / George Gissing / T. FISHER / UNWIN, PATERNOSTER / SQUARE. MDCCCXCV
Everything is printed in black, except 'Autonym Library' which is in rose pink.

Back cover Printed in black: [a device] / *COPYRIGHT EDITION.* / This *COLLECTION MAY* / *BE INTRODUCED INTO ALL* / *EUROPEAN COUNTRIES AND* / *BRITISH COLONIES.*

XVI c

FIRST AMERICAN EDITION

Sleeping Fires / BY / GEORGE GISSING / AUTHOR OF / EVE'S RANSOM, THE ODD WOMEN, / DENZIL QUARRIER, / IN THE YEAR OF JUBILEE, ETC. / [publisher's stamp] / NEW YORK / D. APPLETON AND COMPANY / 1896

Collation [1]–14⁸; 112 leaves (17.55 × 10.4); [i–iv] 1–211 [212]

Contents [i] halftitle: Sleeping Fires [ii] blank [iii] titlepage [iv] copyright: COPYRIGHT, 1895, / BY D. APPLETON AND COMPANY. 1–211 text, on 211: THE END. [212] blank
In some copies eight pages of advertisement have been sewn in at the end.

Binding Spine, and boards at front and back, covered in apple-green medium weave cloth. Cream endpapers.

Front cover At top left is a circle stamped in silver. A dark green-black band is knotted over it to form a clover shape. The title is stamped in silver, within the circle, the word SLEEPING at the top, following the curvature of the circle and, similarly, the word FIRES at the bottom. At the bottom right hand corner is stamped in silver: GEORGE GISSING

Spine At the top, in silver: SLEEPING / FIRES / [short rule] / GISSING At the bottom, again in silver: APPLETONS

Back cover Plain.

PUBLICATION

In the course of a period during which he for the most part wrote short stories, Gissing temporarily lowered his standards and wrote at least two novels in response to direct requests from publishers. *Sleeping Fires* was one of these: he later referred to it as that 'paltry little book of mine.' The undated contract with Fisher Unwin specified a fee of £150 for a 30,000 word novel, which according to the *Diary* Gissing wrote rapidly between mid-January and 1 March 1895 and sent off immediately. On 13 March 1895, he wrote: 'Today I am sending you my story *Sleeping Fires*. It is a type-written copy, with a few MS additions. The typing is reckoned, I see, at 33,000 words, & what I have added will make, perhaps, two or three thousand words' (*Berg*).

In passing it is interesting to note that this is an instance of the publisher's reports having survived. The first reader called the book 'a bad bargain,' even 'if the name did sell a few extra thousand copies,' and advised the publisher 'that a strong effort ought to be made to get good work out of him.' The second reader, on the other hand, said that the book was 'not a pot-boiler' but was the 'sincere outcome of Mr. Gissing's convictions,' holding 'a logical position in his works.' Despite this disagreement, *Sleeping Fires* was published in December 1895, the hardback selling at 2/- and the paperback at 1/6.

XVII a

THE WHIRLPOOL

FIRST EDITION

THE WHIRLPOOL / BY / GEORGE GISSING / [publisher's stamp] / LONDON / LAWRENCE AND BULLEN, LTD. / 16 HENRIETTA STREET, COVENT GARDEN, W.C. / 1897

Collation $[\pi]^2$A–2E^{8}2F^4[2G–2H]^8; 230 leaves (19.3 × 12.8); [i–iv] [1]–453 [454–6] [1]–32

Contents [i] halftitle: THE WHIRLPOOL [ii] publisher's notice: *BY THE SAME AUTHOR* / THE UNCLASSED / THE EMANCIPATED / DENZIL QUARRIER / THE ODD WOMEN / IN THE YEAR OF JUBILEE / EVE'S RANSOM / [iii] titlepage [iv] imprint: *Printed by* BALLANTYNE, HANSON & CO / *At the Ballantyne Press* [1]–453 text, on 453: THE END / *Printed by* BALLANTYNE, HANSON & CO. / *Edinburgh and London* [454–6] blank [1]–32 publisher's advertisements

Binding Spine, and boards at front and back, covered in deep maroon cloth. Cream endpapers.

Front cover At top left is stamped in gilt: THE WHIRLPOOL At bottom right is stamped in gilt: GEORGE GISSING

Spine At the top is stamped in gilt and framed by narrow gilt lines: THE / WHIRLPOOL Beneath the frame is stamped, also in gilt: GEORGE / GISSING At the bottom is stamped in gilt and framed by narrow gilt lines: LAWRENCE & BULLEN

Back cover Plain.

PUBLICATION

One of the new novels that Gissing began to think about in 1895 may have been *The Whirlpool*. On 23 February 1896 he told Bertz: 'Very, very slowly,

I shape the details of a new book' (*Bertz* 214). In all probability, this 'new book' was the one he tentatively called 'Benedict's Household': there is disagreement about whether it was an early version of *The Whirlpool* or not. At all events, *Diary* entries indicate that the novel in its present form was written between 25 August 1896 and 18 December 1896. Gissing sent the manuscript to Lawrence & Bullen almost immediately. The novel was published on 6 April 1897.

Contrary to Gissing's expectations the novel proved relatively successful. In May 1897 he told Bertz that it was selling better than any of his earlier books. 'The first edition of 2000 copies is just being exhausted, and a second 2000 is in the press. Moreover, 1500 copies were printed for Australia' (*Bertz* 230). The second impression was dated 1897 and called 'second edition' on the titlepage. The American edition published by Stokes also did well. There were at least four impressions after the first edition, referred to on the titlepage as second, third, fourth, and fifth edition and all dated 1897.

THE MANUSCRIPT

The manuscript of *The Whirlpool*, which is in the Huntington Library, is a fair copy which carries the printers' thumbprints and the compositors' names. The pagination is continuous from 1 to 180 with only one break: p 82 is missing. Its omission does not, however, result in a break in sense. There are few major corrections to the manuscript and the density of minor changes is not great. Interest in the manuscript derives from the fact that Gissing accepted the publisher's request or demand that the equivalent of 10 pages should be deleted from the proofs, though not with equanimity if one is to judge by the letter Gissing wrote to Bullen on 8 February 1896: 'By Nox Erebus! but your black avised proof startled me at first. However, I find you are quite right: most of what you have blotted out is surplusage. Not all, though; I have been obliged to restore a few lines here & there – points of character or bits of colour I could not bring myself to give up. The difference between your revise & mine does not exceed, I think, some fifty lines' (*Berg*). No one appears to have studied the consequent difference between the manuscript and the first edition.

XVIII a

HUMAN ODDS AND ENDS

FIRST EDITION

HUMAN ODDS AND ENDS / STORIES AND SKETCHES / BY / GEORGE GISSING / [publisher's design] / LONDON / LAWRENCE AND BULLEN, LTD. / 16 HENRIETTA STREET, COVENT GARDEN / 1898

Collation [A]⁴B–W⁸X²; 158 leaves (19 × 12.5); [i–viii] [1]–308

Contents [i–ii] blank [iii] halftitle: HUMAN ODDS AND ENDS [iv] advertisement of books by same author [v] titlepage [vi] imprint: PRINTED BY SPOTTISWOODE AND CO., NEW-STREET SQUARE / LONDON [vii–viii, numbered vi] contents [1]–19 text of 'Comrades in Arms' 20–37 text of 'The Justice and the Vagabond' 38–55 text of 'The Firebrand' 56–73 text of 'An Inspiration' 74–91 text of 'The Poet's Portmanteau' 92–110 text of 'The Day of Silence' 111–32 text of 'In Honour Bound' 133–54 text of 'The Prize Lodger' 155–75 text of 'Our Mr. Jupp' 176–82 text of 'The Medicine Man' 183–90 text of 'Raw Material' 191–6 text of 'Two Collectors' 197–202 text of 'An Old Maid's Triumph' 203–9 text of 'The Invincible Curate' 210–17 text of 'The Toast of Yarmouth' 218–24 text of 'A Well-Meaning Man' 225–30 text of 'A Song of Sixpence' 231–7 text of 'A Profitable Weakness' 238–43 text of 'The Beggar's Nurse' 244–50 text of 'Transplanted' 251–6 text of 'A Parent's Feelings' 257–62 text of 'Lord Dunfield' 263–9 text of 'A Little Woman from Lancashire' 270–6 text of 'In No-man's Land' 277–83 text of 'At High Pressure' 284–9 text of 'A Conversion' 290–5 text of 'A Free Woman' 296–302 text of 'A Son of the Soil' 303–8 text of 'Out of the Fashion'

Binding Purple-brown cloth on boards, ribbed vertically. Endpapers plain.

Front cover Stamped in gilt: HUMAN ODDS AND ENDS / GEORGE GISSING

Spine Stamped in gilt and with the title and the publisher's names enclosed in a simple rectangle: HUMAN / ODDS / AND / ENDS / GEORGE / GISSING / LAWRENCE AND BULLEN

Back cover Plain.

XIX a

CHARLES DICKENS

FIRST EDITION

Charles Dickens / A Critical Study / By / GEORGE GISSING / LONDON / BLACKIE & SON, LIMITED, 50 OLD BAILEY, E.C. / GLASGOW AND DUBLIN / 1898

Collation [A]⁸B–P⁸Q²; 122 leaves (18.4 × 12.0); i–v [vi] [7]–244

Contents [i] halftitle: *The Victorian Era Series* / Charles Dickens [ii] blank [iii] titlepage [iv] chronology of Dickens' publications [v]–vi contents [7]–244 text, on 244 at foot: PRINTED BY BLACKIE AND SON, LIMITED, GLASGOW.

Pasted in at the beginning is a single leaf advertising the series.

Binding Spine, and boards at front and back, covered in maroon cloth. Cream endpapers.

Front cover Vertical borders consisting of three horizontal lines at the top and four at the bottom printed in black, and between them, with a fairly elaborate crest at top left: THE VICTORIAN ERA SERIES / CHARLES DICKENS

Spine The borders, now in gilt, are continued from the front cover and between them, also stamped in gilt: CHARLES / DICKENS / [rule] / GISSING / BLACKIE & SON LTD.

Back cover Plain.

AMERICAN FIRST EDITION

Charles Dickens / *A Critical Study* / By / GEORGE GISSING / Author of Denzil Quarrier / In the Year of Jubilee / [device] / New York / Dodd, Mead and Company / 1898

Collation $[\pi]^2 1^6 2$–$20^8 21^2$; 162 leaves (19.2 × 13.0); [i–vi] 1–318

Contents [i] halftitle: Charles Dickens [ii] blank [iii] titlepage [iv] copyright statement and imprint: *Copyright, 1898,* / BY DODD, MEAD AND COMPANY. / *University Press:* / JOHN WILSON AND SON, CAMBRIDGE, U.S.A. [v] contents [vi] blank 1–318 text

Binding Spine, and boards at front and back, covered in stiff grey paper. White endpapers.

Front cover Within a stamped framework of two black and one red line, with a tulip-shaped design at centre and the designer's initials at bottom right, stamped in gilt: CHARLES / DICKENS and stamped in red: By / GEORGE GISSING

Spine Stamped in gilt: CHARLES / DICKENS / [design] / GISSING Stamped in black at the bottom: DODD, MEAD / & COMPANY Between the title and the name of the publisher are two rectangles each made of a double black line.

Back cover Plain.

PUBLICATIONS

Anyone writing about Gissing's work on Dickens must be indebted to Pierre Coustillas' little book *Gissing's Writings on Dickens* (London: Enitharmon Press 1969), in which much of the available information has been collected.

Essentially there were two spells of work, the first resulting in *Charles Dickens: A Critical Study*, and the second in a collection of prefaces which in North America were eventually published as *Critical Studies of the Works of Charles Dickens* and in England as *The Immortal Dickens*. With each of these two works other publications, though not books, are associated and are mentioned either here or in xxx. Nonetheless, Gissing was occupied continuously with Dickens during the last years of his life and Dr Coustillas adopted the correct approach in considering them together.

The book described here came first. Just after Christmas 1896, an old acquaintance of Gissing, Holland Rose, asked him to write a book on Dickens for a series – the Victorian Era Series – which was to be published by Blackie. Though he agreed, he did not start immediately. He was by this time seriously ill, during the first six months of 1897 was under doctor's orders, and for part of the time lived in Budleigh Salterton by himself in an attempt to recover his health. There seems also to have been an attempt to recover family equilibrium, for the Gissings had a long summer holiday in Yorkshire. In the autumn, however, there had been a further deterioration on both counts; Algernon took Walter to Wakefield, Gissing left Edith and Alfred on 17 September, and on 22 September he left England for the winter. He travelled almost directly to Siena, where he immediately settled to the work on Dickens. On 23 October he told his agent, Colles, that he had done half and a letter dated 6 November announcing the completion of the book was quickly followed by a parcel, two days later, containing the complete manuscript (*Pforzheimer*). On 9 December 1897 he returned the corrected typescript to Colles and on 2 January 1898 despatched the corrected proofs of the English edition to Dodd, Mead. He had kept to his understanding with Holland Rose and completed the book within twelve months.

The agreement specified a royalty of 10 per cent on the first 4000 and 15 per cent on subsequent copies sold, with an advance of £30. Gissing's 'Minute of Agreement' with Blackie, witnessed by Catherine and Algernon Gissing, is in the Beinecke Library. Later Colles sold the American rights to Dodd, Mead for £50, though Gissing retained the English copyright. Since the book was relatively successful, it seems unfortunate that Gissing should not have received more for it: there is no evidence of royalty payment during his lifetime. A few years later he sold the British rights to Blackie for £50 to permit the book to be used as part of Gresham's Imperial Edition of Dickens' works which was published in 1902. His letter to Gabrielle Fleury dated 16 January 1902 shows that he corrected proofs for this new edition, which thus provides the definitive text of *Charles Dickens: A Critical Study* (*Fleury* 147). A second impression was issued in 1904 and later a 'colonial edition': in *NBL* there is a record of an issue in India by Blackie dated 1928. The book was in fact reissued many times both in England and in North America.

THE MANUSCRIPT

The manuscript of *Charles Dickens*, which is a fair copy, is in the Pforzheimer Library.

XX a

THE TOWN TRAVELLER

FIRST EDITION

THE / TOWN TRAVELLER / BY / GEORGE GISSING / METHUEN & CO. / 36 ESSEX STREET, W.C. / LONDON / 1898

Collation [A]–U^8; 160 leaves (19.0 × 12.7); [i]–vi 1–313 [314] [1]–40

Contents [i] halftitle: THE TOWN TRAVELLER [ii] publisher's notice: BY THE SAME AUTHOR / [short rule] / THE UNCLASSED / IN THE YEAR OF JUBILEE / THE ODD WOMEN / EVE'S RANSOM / THE WHIRLPOOL / BORN IN EXILE [iii] titlepage [iv] blank [v]–vi contents 1–313 text, on 313: THE END [314] imprint: PLYMOUTH: / WILLIAM BRENDON AND SONS, / PRINTERS. [1]–40 publisher's advertisement in some copies.

Binding Spine, and boards at front and back, covered in scarlet cloth. Cream endpapers.

Front cover About the middle of the right half, stamped in gilt and framed by narrow gilt lines forming an upright rectangle: THE / TOWN / TRAVELLER / BY / GEORGE / GISSING

Spine Near the top, stamped in gilt and framed by gilt lines: THE / TOWN / TRAVELLER / GEORGE / GISSING At the bottom stamped in gilt and framed by gilt lines: METHUEN

Back cover Plain.

XX b

THE AMERICAN FIRST EDITION

THE / TOWN TRAVELLER / BY / GEORGE GISSING / *Author of 'The Whirlpool,' 'In the Year of Jubilee,' / 'The Unclassed,' Etc.* / [small device] / NEW YORK / FREDERICK A. STOKES COMPANY / PUBLISHERS

Collation [1–19]⁸; 152 leaves (18.7 × 12.7); [i–vi] 1–293 [294–8]

Contents [i] halftitle: THE TOWN TRAVELLER [ii] blank [iii] titlepage [iv] copyright and imprint: COPYRIGHT, 1898, / BY FREDERICK A. STOKES COMPANY. / [short rule] / *All Rights Reserved.* / PRESSWORK BY / THE UNIVERSITY PRESS, CAMBRIDGE, U.S.A. [v] contents [vi] blank 1–293 text, on 293: THE END. [294–8] blank

Binding Spine, and boards at front and back, covered in avocado green, medium weave cloth. Cream endpapers.

Front cover The whole front cover is taken up with relatively complex design blind-stamped in black, red, and light green, the predominant feature of which is a picture of a man in top hat and overcoat with astrakahn collar walking past a shop. Over the door of the shop are the words: CLOVER. CHINA. At the bottom left of the picture are the initials: GWE. Beneath the picture, in a black rectangle, is: The TOWN / TRAVELLER / by / GEORGE GISSING

Spine Between a simple design at the top and a set of horizontal lines in red and black at the bottom: The / TOWN / TRAV- / ELLER / by / GISSING / STOKES

Back cover Plain.

PUBLICATION

It is said that, uncharacteristically, Gissing wrote *The Town Traveller* merely to earn money as quickly as possible, but he evidently had a prior understanding with Colles about the placing of a serial. 'At last I am able to redeem my promise to you.

I have written a story called *The Town Traveller* – a comedy of the lower middle classes. Length, some 80,000 words.

Now I could let you have the first half of this at once; the second half I want to keep for a little more revision' (*Pforzheimer*). Colles responded quickly, for Gissing in fact sent him the first part on 27 June and the second part on 15 July.

A little time was to pass, however, before an agreement was reached. Methuen's first offer was too low. Gissing wanted either the cash payment that went with a serial or a reasonable advance against royalties. On 28 January 1898 he told Colles: 'I wrote *The Town Traveller* expressly for serial use. If it cannot find admission to the Magazines, then I will either withdraw it altogether, or have a *considerably more important advance* than this of Methuen's' (*Pforzheimer*). Gissing's attitude was in part a cynical one, for he said repeatedly during this period of his life that the way things appeared in magazines did not matter since no one whose judgement he would respect ever read them.

Nonetheless his resistance had a straightforward commercial result: Methuen proposed better terms. Colles had negotiated an advance of £250 against royalties from Methuen and one of £100 from Stokes for an American edition. Though Gissing remained apprehensive about the disposal of rights, and was later upset when he learnt that Colles had sold the translation rights for £10, he was on the whole satisfied, since he knew that the book was a poor one. 'A total advance of £350,' he wrote blandly, 'is not at all a bad beginning' (*Pforzheimer*). There is a useful note on Gissing's contract with Stokes for *The Town Traveller* in *The Gissing Newsletter*, Vol. VII, Number 4, October 1971. A little later Colles arranged for a Canadian issue by Morang of Toronto from which Gissing was to receive five cents per copy sold. This Canadian issue, dated 1899 and charmingly registered for copyright purposes by the Minister of Agriculture, was from the American not the English first edition.

The production of the book proceeded without delay. On 11 May 1898 the complete corrected typescript was returned to Pinker; proofs were corrected during June; and the book was published on 29 August, rather more than a year after it had been written. The novel was added to Methuen's Colonial Library and issued on cheaper paper and with either buff wrappers or blue-green cloth in the same year. Later, probably in 1902, it was reissued in a sixpenny edition.

THE MANUSCRIPT

The complete manuscript of *The Town Traveller* in the Beinecke is the one used by the typist in the preparation of final copy. The twenty-seven chapters correspond to those of the first edition and there are few corrections of more than a sentence or two. Changes in pagination perhaps indicate that Gissing modified the book or patched it up as he was making the fair copy, but it is without evident critical interest.

XXI a

THE CROWN OF LIFE

FIRST EDITION

THE / CROWN OF LIFE / BY / GEORGE GISSING / METHUEN & CO. / 36 ESSEX STREET, W.C. / LONDON / 1899

Collation $[\pi]^2 1$–$20^8 21^6$; 188 leaves (19.0 × 12.6); [i–iv] [1]–329 [330–2] [1]–40

Contents [i] halftitle: THE CROWN OF LIFE [ii] publisher's notice: BY THE SAME AUTHOR / THE UNCLASSED / IN THE YEAR OF JUBILEE / THE ODD WOMEN / EVE'S RANSOM / THE WHIRLPOOL / BORN IN EXILE / THE TOWN TRAVELLER [iii] titlepage [iv] blank [1]–329 text, on 329: THE END [330] imprint: PRINTED BY / MORRISON AND GIBB LIMITED, / EDINBURGH [331–2] blank [1]–40 publisher's advertisement sewn in a single gathering into some copies.

Binding Spine, and boards at front and back, covered in light red cloth. Endpapers very light cream almost identical in shade to paper.

Front cover About the middle of the right half of this, stamped in gilt and framed by narrow gilt lines forming an upright rectangle: THE / CROWN / OF / LIFE / BY / GEORGE GISSING

Spine Near the top, stamped in gilt and framed by gilt lines: THE CROWN / OF / LIFE / GEORGE GISSING At the bottom, in gilt and framed by gilt lines: METHUEN

Back cover Plain.

XXI b

FIRST AMERICAN EDITION

THE / CROWN OF LIFE / BY / GEORGE GISSING / AUTHOR OF 'THE WHIRLPOOL,' 'THE UNCLASSED,' / 'THE TOWN TRAVELLER,' ETC. / [a device consisting of a small black leaf on a stem] / NEW YORK / FREDERICK A. STOKES COMPANY / 1899

Collation $[\pi]^3 1$–$22^8 23^4$; 182 leaves (18.65×12.5); [i–iv] [1]–360

Contents [i] halftitle: THE CROWN OF LIFE [ii] blank [iii] titlepage [iv] copyright and imprint: *Copyright, 1899,* / BY FREDERICK A. STOKES COMPANY. / [short rule] / *All rights reserved.* / University Press: / JOHN WILSON AND SON, CAMBRIDGE, U.S.A. [1]–360 text, on 360: THE END.

Binding Spine, and boards at front and back, covered in green cloth. Cream endpapers.

Front cover Stamped in black at all four edges a scrolled border 65 mm. wide and formed from an arrangement of stems and leaves. Within this frame, at the top and stamped in gilt: THE CROWN / OF LIFE A little beneath the title is a crown and below that a flowering plant with one big blossom at the top. Crown and plant are stamped in dark brown. A little below is stamped in gilt: GEORGE GISSING

Spine At the top and bottom edges is the same brown scrolled design as on the front cover, though not continuous with it. Beneath the scroll is a three-leafed device, in dark brown, and below that, the title in gilt: THE / CROWN / OF / LIFE / [short wavy line] / GISSING The drawing of the crown and flowery plant is repeated in dark brown. At the bottom near the lower border is stamped in gilt: STOKES

Back cover Plain.

PUBLICATION

Gissing wrote *The Crown of Life* during the winter of 1898–9, between Gabrielle Fleury's return to Paris in October 1898 after a brief visit to Dorking and 17 January 1899 when he told Bertz the book was finished. The *Diary* shows that he had begun to think seriously about the book in July 1898, but for various reasons he was not free to start it immediately: early in September he still referred to it as 'the book I am going to write' (*Bertz* 251). His final parting from his second wife, Edith, occurred in September, however, so that with both boys at school and in the care of others he could settle down to write his 'peace' book, which was also a kind of love story.

Pinker began to negotiate for the book before very much of it was written, since despite Gissing's apprehension about leaving Lawrence & Bullen he had in fact given Pinker *carte blanche* to obtain the best terms possible. The novel was sent to Pinker to be typed as it was written, with the result that Gissing was correcting the typescript of early parts of the novel at the same time as he was writing the concluding chapters. On 12 January 1899 he thanked Pinker for eleven chapters of the novel in typescript: 'I shall have to finish the work before I begin to revise, but it will only be a few days delay' (*Pforzheimer*). But on 16 January he mailed the last three chapters of manuscript; on 17 January he told Bertz he had finished the novel (*Bertz* 254); and on the following day he wrote to Pinker again: 'Today I post to you the whole of the typescript, revised' (*Pforzheimer*).

Gissing was mildly upset about what he regarded as a delay in the publishing of a book he had written so rapidly. 'Alas!' he wrote to Bertz on 31 March 1899, 'My novel is put off until September – partly because the present season is over-crowded with books, partly because *The Town Traveller* is still selling. I think it is a mistake, the story being so opportune; but publishers are *always* making mistakes' (*Bertz* 259). Actually Gissing did not fully understand that, having sold the American rights, he was not in a position to insist upon simultaneous publication. Two typescripts had been produced, the top copy and the carbon, one for the English the other for the American publisher, and since he corrected both the process took time. Pinker had in any case obtained reasonable terms. He received an advance against royalties of £300 on the English edition and £100 on the American. The English royalties were to be 20 per cent on a first issue of 2500 copies to be sold at 6/- and 25 per cent on all subsequent copies. In addition Gissing was to receive a 15 per cent royalty on the American edition and 4d. for each copy of the colonial issue sold. The dates on the advertisement pages of September 1899 and November 1899 in the two copies of the first edition at Yale probably indicate not that the novel was quickly reissued but that not all copies had been bound at the outset.

Gissing corrected various batches of proofs for both editions during June, July, and August and the novel was published, in England, on 23 October. It was issued simultaneously in Canada and distributed by W.J. Gage and, a few years later, in 1905, Methuen reissued it as number LXV of 'The Novelist Series.' This, too, derives directly from the first edition.

THE MANUSCRIPT

The manuscript of *The Crown of Life*, which is now in the Huntington Library, is the fair copy used by Pinker's typist. In other words, a corrected typescript stands between the manuscript and the first edition. Nonetheless the difference between the manuscript fair copy and the first edition is slight; Florio, previously a Greek, becomes an Italian and a minor episode concerning a letter is eliminated.

XXII a

OUR FRIEND THE CHARLATAN

FIRST EDITION

OUR FRIEND / THE CHARLATAN / BY GEORGE GISSING / WITH ILLUSTRATIONS BY LAUNCELOT SPEED / LONDON / CHAPMAN AND HALL, LD. / 1901

Collation [A]^{6}B–DD^{8}EE^6; 218 leaves (18.9 × 13.0); [i–viii] [1]–[425] [426–8]

Contents [i] halftitle: OUR FRIEND / THE CHARLATAN [ii] advertisement of *By the Ionian Sea* [iii] titlepage [iv] blank [v] prefatory note over the author's initials and dated 1901 at St. Honoré en Morvan [vi] blank [vii] list of illustrations [viii] blank [1]–[425] text, on [425]: THE END. / [short rule] / *Richard Clay & Sons, Limited, London & Bungay.* [426] publisher's advertisements [427–8] blank

Binding Spine, and boards at front and back, covered in navy-blue cloth. Cream endpapers.

Front cover On top half of cover, scroll work stamped in gilt to form a shape approximating that of a butterfly with wings stretched out, and within this, in gilt: OUR · FRIEND / THE · CHARLATAN / GEORGE · GISSING

Spine The same butterfly shape as above, elongated to fit on the spine, stamped in gilt. Stamped within this, in gilt: OUR / FRIEND / THE / CHARLATAN / GEORGE / GISSING At the bottom, also stamped in gilt: CHAPMAN & HALL

Back cover Plain.

Binding variant Spine, and boards at front and back, covered in stiff green paper. Beige endpapers.

Front cover A frame printed in red and consisting of a border approximately 1 cm. from all four edges is divided by two horizontal lines, the one towards the top and the other towards the bottom. In the top rectangle is printed in black: Our Friend [device] / [device] the Charlatan. At centre is an illustration. In the lower rectangle is printed in black: By GEORGE GISSING

Spine Within a simple framework similar to that on the front cover and printed in black: OUR FRIEND / THE / CHARLATAN / BY / GEORGE / GISSING / 2/- / CHAPMAN & HALL

Back cover Plain.

Whether this binding variant should be referred to as such or be regarded, rather, as a cheaper reissue of the first edition is perhaps unimportant: in the same year a colonial issue was prepared from the same plates and in 1906 a sixpenny reprint.

XXII b

AMERICAN FIRST EDITION

OUR FRIEND THE CHARLATAN / *A NOVEL* / BY / GEORGE GISSING / [publisher's stamp] / NEW YORK / HENRY HOLT AND COMPANY / 1901

Collation [1]–25^8; 200 leaves (18.7 × 12.6); [i–iv] [1]–386 [387–96]

Contents [i] titlepage [ii] copyright: Copyright, 1901, / BY / HENRY HOLT & CO. [iii] prefatory note by G.G. dated Aug. 29, 1900 at St. Honoré. Nièvre [iv] blank [1]–386 text, on 386: THE END. [387–96] publisher's advertisement, at the foot of each page: [on left] HENRY HOLT & CO. [on right] 29 West 23rd Street / New York

Binding Spine, and boards at front and back, covered in blue cloth. Cream endpapers.

Front cover Within a dark blue frame are two horizontal decorative borders, one at the top, the other at the bottom, both with a dark blue background and with a pattern in a lighter blue. In the space between these two borders is stamped in dark blue: OUR FRIEND / THE CHARLATAN / [short rule] / GISSING.

Spine Stamped in blue: OUR / FRIEND / THE / CHARLATAN / [ornamental design of horizontal lines and intervening shading] / HENRY HOLT & CO.

PUBLICATION

The writing of *Our Friend the Charlatan* was interrupted during the winter of 1899–1900 when Gissing decided to write *Among the Prophets*, a book which was about 'the restless seeking for a *new religion*, which lends people Theosophy, Spiritualism, and things still more foolish' and which he in fact finished and sent to Pinker, though it was never published. *Our Friend the Charlatan* was started late in September and the writing went well enough for him to tell Pinker about it on 2 October 1899 and Bertz on 22 October 1899. It was in November that he put it aside, probably after about six weeks' work.

When in the spring of 1900 Gissing ordered Pinker to burn the typescript of *Among the Prophets*, it seems that he did not make a fresh start on *Our Friend the Charlatan*, which would have been consistent with his earlier practice, but simply picked up the threads from where he had left them. This was in May. Though Gissing was busy with other things, there were no further interruptions and by 29 August 1900 the book was finished.

At this time Gissing was living at St Honoré-les-Bains near Nèvers and once again he left the practical arrangement for the book to Pinker, his agent. Time passed as Pinker tried to receive favourable terms both for a serial issue in England and for simultaneous publication in book form in England and North America. Eventually, Chapman and Hall offered £350 for the seven-year lease of the copyright and Henry Holt £150 for the American rights, though this latter amount was reduced when a disagreement arose about the date of publication. The memorandum of agreement with Holt, dated 22 May 1901, in fact specifies an advance of £100 and a 15 per cent royalty for a seven-year lease of the copyright. It was not until the early spring of 1901, when Gissing was correcting the typescript for the American edition and the proofs of the English, that he changed the name of the book from *The Coming Man* to *Our Friend the Charlatan*. The corrected proofsheets of the English edition, or rather the corrected serial pages, are in the possession of Mme D. le Mallier.

The novel was published in May in England (at six shillings) and in June in North America, without having appeared in serial form.

THE MANUSCRIPT

The autograph manuscript of *Our Friend the Charlatan* is now in the Alexander Turnbull Library in Wellington, New Zealand.

XXIII a

BY THE IONIAN SEA

FIRST EDITION

BY THE IONIAN SEA / NOTES OF A RAMBLE IN / SOUTHERN ITALY / BY / GEORGE GISSING / WITH EIGHT ILLUSTRATIONS IN COLOUR BY LEO DE LITTROW / AND OTHERS IN BLACK AND WHITE / LONDON / CHAPMAN AND HALL, LD. / 1901

Collation [A]⁴B–L⁸M⁴; 88 leaves (25 × 19); [i–viii] [1]–168

Contents [i] halftitle: BY THE IONIAN SEA [ii] blank [iii] titlepage [iv] blank [v] contents [vi] blank [vii] list of illustrations [viii] blank [1]–168 text, on 168: THE END. / [short rule] / *Richard Clay & Sons, Limited, London & Bungay. / Coloured Illustrations printed by / Vincent Brooks, Day & Son, Ltd.*
9 illustrations, each of which is covered by a leaf of thin paper, have been pasted in.

Binding Spine, and boards at front and back, covered in ivory white cloth. Endpapers of the same white paper as the rest of the book.
Front cover Stamped in gilt at top left: BY [design of scroll work] / THE IONIAN / SEA [device repeated] / GEORGE GISSING

Spine Stamped in gilt: BY THE / IONIAN / SEA / GEORGE / GISSING / CHAPMAN & HALL

Back cover Plain.

XXIII b

REISSUE OF THE FIRST EDITION

The first edition of *By the Ionian Sea* was reissued in green cloth, with cream endpapers and on a slightly smaller page (22.7 × 17.2). Though as a reissue it carried the original date, 1901, there is some doubt about when it in act appeared. The Beinecke has a copy into which has been inserted a letter on the letterhead of Elkin Matthews.

'Now about the IONIAN SEA book, this was published during the summer of 1901 and advertised in the form only for 16/-. I am quite sure this was the white cloth issue. Similar copies in green (and I think also in red) are almost certainly a cheaper binding put on the sheets of copies which had failed to sell at the time of publication. I believe they are several years later than 1901. I have no evidence of this at all but I have had the two forms of the book side by side and the coloured cloth copies are so much meaner and cheaper in appearance and I am sure this is the explanation.'

In one of the copies inspected, there is a portrait of Gissing between [ii] and [iii] with the inscription: THE LATE MR. GEORGE GISSING / whose death was the worst blow suffered by English letters in 1904. Of course, Gissing died in 1903 but it seems likely that Chapman & Hall reissued the book after, and perhaps as a result of, his death.

XXIII c

THE REISSUE OF 1905

In 1905 a second impression of the reissue appeared, which can most easily be identified by its titlepage:
BY THE IONIAN SEA / NOTES OF A RAMBLE IN / SOUTHERN ITALY / BY / GEORGE GISSING / SECOND IMPRESSION / OF / NEW AND CHEAPER EDITION / ILLUSTRATED / LONDON / CHAPMAN AND HALL LD. / 1905
This 'new and cheaper' edition was issued in North America by Scribner, the titlepage reading: BY THE IONIAN SEA / NOTES OF A RAMBLE IN / SOUTHERN ITALY / BY / GEORGE GISSING / ILLUSTRATED / NEW YORK / CHARLES SCRIBNER'S SONS / 1905.

PUBLICATION

Gissing began to plan *By the Ionian Sea* in 1897, though two years were to pass before he actually wrote it. (The implication in *NBL* that the book was written in 1897 is an error – no doubt an inadvertent one.) On 13 September 1897 he told Bertz of his decision to go to Italy. 'I take ship at Naples (the Messina Steamer) for *Paola*, on the Calabrian coast, where these steamers call. (This is the town of S. Francesco di Paola, you know.) Thence I can travel by diligence, across the mountains, to Cosenza, where Alaric died. Here I touch the railway again, and with its help I mean to explore all (or nearly all) Magna

Graecia, which may possibly yield me material for a book of travel sketches. The Editor of the *Daily Chronicle* has asked me to send him anything I think likely to suit the paper. I shall buy photographs, and make rough drawings, for the illustrations of my proposed book' (*Bertz* 236). His travels went more or less as planned, but when he returned to England the following spring, he had other books to complete and domestic affairs to attend to. Entries in the *Diary* indicate that the book was written between 29 June and 9 August 1899, the 'concluding portion' being sent to Pinker on 13 August.

Though Gissing was once again anxious to have the immediate payment that would be expected from serial publication, Pinker in fact had difficulty in placing the book. Not until February 1900 was he able to report that the *Fortnightly Review* had offered £120 for the serial rights, which Gissing accepted. Shortly afterwards, Pinker received from Chapman & Hall the offer of £130 for a seven year lease of the copyright, an arrangement which Chapman & Hall had preferred for many years though authors were becoming more and more disinclined to accept it. Gissing, however, did accept it. On 31 May 1900 he replied to Pinker's letter: 'Yes, I will take C & H's £130 for rent of 7 years' English (I presume, English) copyright . . . Of course I am sorry to hear of S. & E's refusal, but not greatly surprised' (*Pforzheimer*). To Bertz he acknowledged that straitened circumstances made it difficult for him to hold out for better terms (*Bertz* 287). Gissing corrected proofs in May 1900, but for various reasons – one being the difficulties encountered in the preparation of the illustrations – the book was not published until June 1901. Its original price was 16/-.

THE MANUSCRIPT

The manuscript of *By the Ionian Sea* is in the Pforzheimer Library.

XXIV a

THE PRIVATE PAPERS OF HENRY RYECROFT

FIRST EDITION

THE PRIVATE PAPERS OF / HENRY RYECROFT / BY / GEORGE GISSING / *Hoc erat in votis* / WESTMINSTER / ARCHIBALD CONSTABLE & CO LTD / 2 WHITEHALL GARDENS / 1903

Collation [A]–U⁸; 160 leaves (18.55 × 12.3); [a–b] [i]–xiv 1–298 1–6

Contents [a–b] blank [i] halftitle: THE PRIVATE PAPERS OF / HENRY RYECROFT [ii] blank [iii] titlepage [iv] imprint: BUTLER & TANNER, / THE SELWOOD PRINTING WORKS, / FROME, AND LONDON. v contents [vi] blank [vii]–xiv preface by G.G. 1 flytitle: SPRING [2] blank 3–75 text [76] blank [77] flytitle: AUTUMN [156] blank 157–222 text [223] flytitle: WINTER [224] blank 225–93 text [294] blank 295–8 index, at foot of 298: Butler & Tanner, The Selwood Printing Works, Frome, and London. 1–6 separately numbered publisher's advertisement.

Binding Spine, and boards at front and back, covered in dark green cloth Cream endpapers.

Front cover A frame of narrow gilt lines runs less than .35 cms from all sides. At the top is stamped in gilt: THE PRIVATE PAPERS OF HENRY RYECROFT / GEORGE GISSING

Spine Stamped in gilt and between rules at top and bottom: THE PRIVATE / PAPERS / OF / HENRY / REYCROFT / GEORGE / GISSING / Constable / Westminster

Back cover Plain.

PUBLICATION

Gissing had brooded over the book that was to become *The Private Papers of Henry Ryecroft* for some fifteen years before he actually wrote it. Even then he revised it at least twice. The first significant revision was in the autumn of 1901 when he returned to France after a period in a sanatorium in Suffolk. As usual he reported his progress to Bertz: 'Meanwhile, I am doing a little work – about two hours every morning. I am engaged upon "An Author at Grass," which I am considerably altering and improving' (*Bertz* 298–9). That was in September 1901.

The placing of the book was left to Pinker, though Gissing urged him to get as good a bargain as possible for the serial and foreign rights. Contrary to the opinion of some critics, there appears to be no direct evidence to support the suggestion that the agent found it difficult to interest a publisher. W.L. Courtney accepted it for the *Fortnightly Review* and its four parts appeared on 1 May, 1 August and 1 November 1902, and 1 February 1903. Gissing received £150 for the serial. Meanwhile Pinker had declined Chapman and Hall's offer of a 20 per cent royalty on the book publication with an advance of £100 and the book then went to Constable, whose terms, however, were the same as Chapman and Hall's. Gissing's contract with Constable was dated 2 July 1902. The book was an instant success when it appeared in January 1903, and new impressions were issued in March, April, and October ·1903, as well as in February and October 1904. As has already been mentioned in the introduction, the extent to which Gissing benefited from the success of the book is debatable.

Constable sold the book in sheets for an American issue of 500 copies by E.P. Dutton and made a further 750 copies available for colonial distribution in green cloth or buff wrappers.

THE MANUSCRIPT

The manuscript of an early version of *The Private Papers of Henry Ryecroft* is in the Pforzheimer. Its relationship to the first edition has been discussed briefly by Pierre Coustillas in his critical edition of the book (*George Gissing: Les Carnets d'Henry Ryecroft*, introduction, traduction et notes par Pierre Coustillas, Aubier-Montaigne 1966).

PART II

Works published after
Gissing's death
which had not appeared
in any form during his lifetime

XXV

WILL WARBURTON

FIRST EDITION

WILL WARBURTON / A ROMANCE OF REAL LIFE / BY / GEORGE GISSING / AUTHOR OF 'THE PRIVATE PAPERS OF HENRY RYECROFT' / 'VERANILDA' 'NEW GRUB STREET' 'DEMOS' ETC / LONDON / ARCHIBALD CONSTABLE & CO LTD / 16, JAMES STREET, HAYMARKET S.W. / 1905

Collation [A]–X⁸[Y]⁸; 176 leaves (18.8 × 12.2); [1–4] 5–332 [333–6] [1]–16

Contents [1] halftitle: WILL WARBURTON [2] advertisement of HENRY RYECROFT and VERANILDA [3] titlepage [4] imprint: BUTLER & TANNER, / THE SELWOOD PRINTING WORKS, FROME, AND LONDON. 5–[333] text, on [333]: THE END / [short rule] / Butler & Tanner, The Selwood Printing Works, Frome, and London [334] blank [335–6] advertisement for VERANILDA and HENRY RYECROFT [1]–16 publisher's advertisement

Binding Spine, and boards at front and back, bound in cherry red cloth. Cream endpapers.

Front cover Near the top are stamped two borders, each consisting of one straight and two wavy lines. In the space between them is stamped in gilt: WILL WARBURTON and a little below the lower border, also in gilt: GEORGE GISSING

Spine The two borders are extended over the spine and again, in between them, is stamped in gilt: WILL / WARBURTON
Below the lower border is: GEORGE / GISSING
At the bottom: CONSTABLE / LONDON

Back cover Plain.

PUBLICATION

Gissing began to think of the novel that become *Will Warburton* during the early part of 1902 when he lived by himself in Arcachon, Gabrielle Fleury having returned to Paris to look after her mother. Recently released from the sanatorium in Suffolk, he felt frustrated by his inability to work. The following winter, however, though he had to proceed much more slowly than had been the custom in the past, he worked at the novel steadily and finished it in March. He left to Pinker the task of finding a publisher both for the serial and for the book publication. Although Gissing corrected the typescript, the novel was not published during his lifetime. It appeared posthumously in June 1905. Pinker had in fact negotiated quite reasonable terms with Constable: Gissing was to receive a royalty of 20 per cent on the first 2500 copies sold, and 25 per cent on subsequent sales.

THE MANUSCRIPT

The manuscript of *Will Warburton*, now in the Berg Collection, is a fair copy which is paginated consistently from [1]–102 and which is of little textual interest, for indeed Gissing corrected the typescript that was produced from it. A pencilled note by Gabrielle Fleury at the end of the MS confirms that it was written at St Jean de Luz in 1902–3.

XXVI

VERANILDA

FIRST EDITION

VERANILDA / *A ROMANCE* / BY / GEORGE GISSING / AUTHOR OF 'THE PRIVATE PAPERS OF / HENRY RYECROFT,' ETC. / London / ARCHIBALD CONSTABLE / AND COMPANY, LTD. / 1904

Collation [a]²[b]⁴A–X⁸Y⁴Z²[AA]⁸; 188 leaves (18.6 × 12.1); [a–b] [i–x] [1]–348 [1]–16

Contents [a–b] blank [i] halftitle: VERANILDA [ii] advertisement of THE PRIVATE PAPERS OF HENRY RYECROFT, with excerpts from reviews [iii] titlepage [iv] imprint: Edinburgh: T. and A. CONSTABLE, Printers to His Majesty [v–vii] introduction by Frederic Harrison [viii] blank [ix–x] contents [1]–348 text, on 348: [four asterisks] / [short rule] / Printed by T. and A. CONSTABLE, Printers to His Majesty / at the Edinburgh University Press [1]–16 publisher's advertisement

Binding Spine, and boards at front and back, covered in cherry red cloth. Cream endpapers.

Front cover Blind-stamped near the top two borders, each formed by one straight and two wavy lines. In the space between, stamped in gilt: VERANILDA A little below the lower border, also in gilt: GEORGE GISSING

Spine The two borders are extended over the spine on which is stamped in gilt: VERANILDA / GEORGE / GISSING / CONSTABLE / LONDON

Back cover Plain.

PUBLICATION

'I am beginning my historical novel (Italy in the Sixth Century), of which I spoke to you long ago. I have made a laborious study of the period, and feel able to treat it; a month's toil has resulted in a detailed plan of the book, but whether circumstances will allow me to write it, I cannot say' (*Letters* 373). These sentences were part of a letter to Clara Collet on 27 December 1900: in the *Diary* he recorded the beginning of *Veranilda* on Christmas Day. He had indeed made a laborious preparation for the novel. He began to think about it as far back as 1895; he had it in mind when he travelled in Italy in 1897, for example when he stayed in Monte Cassino in the December of that year; and while still busy on his other projects he began to anticipate the actual labour of writing the book, as in his letter to Gabrielle Fleury dated 4 April 1899: 'For my Roman novel we must try to be permanently settled, as I shall need to have a lot of books about me' (*Fleury* 127). Circumstances, however, did indeed make the labour a slow one: his health deteriorated; the task of finding a place in the south of France in which he could settle with Gabrielle Fleury was, for him, an onerous one; and still more work intervened, in particular the short story called 'Topham's Chance.' Though the novel was accepted for publication in November 1903, Gissing died before completing it: he had five chapters still to write.

On 3 November 1903 he had written to Pinker: 'I am posting to you, registered, the MS of *22 chapters* of *Veranilda* – 87 MS pages . . . There will probably be about 50 more pages of MS' (*Pforzheimer*). On the strength of this, Pinker arranged for a contract to be drawn up with Constable, by which Gissing was to receive a royalty of 25 per cent after 2500 copies sold at 6/- and 4d. on each copy in the Colonial Edition. The incomplete novel was published posthumously in October 1904 and a second impression was issued in the same year.

An American stereotype edition was published in 1905 by E.P. Dutton.

Pierre Coustillas in his article 'The Stormy Publication of Gissing's *Veranilda*' (*Bulletin of the New York Public Library*, 72(9) November 1968, pp 588–610), has described the dispute that arose because of the Gissing family's objection to the preface for the book written by H.G. Wells. A new preface was in the end written by Frederic Harrison while Wells published his in the *Monthly Review* for August 1904. (The Wells' preface has been reprinted as an appendix to Gettmann's *George Gissing and H.G. Wells.*) Neither the prefaces nor the controversy have a direct bearing on *Veranilda* itself.

THE MANUSCRIPT

The manuscript of *Veranilda* is in the Pforzheimer Library. A partial early draft is in the possession of C.C. Kohler.

XXVII

THE HOUSE / OF COBWEBS / AND OTHER STORIES / BY / GEORGE GISSING / TO WHICH IS PREFIXED / THE WORK OF GEORGE GISSING / AN INTRODUCTORY SURVEY / BY THOMAS SECCOMBE / LONDON / ARCHIBALD CONSTABLE / AND COMPANY, LTD. / 1906

Collation [a]⁸b–c⁸d⁴A–S⁸T⁶; 178 leaves (18.8 × 12); [i–lvi] [1]–300

Contents [i] halftitle: THE HOUSE OF COBWEBS [ii] blank [iii] titlepage [iv] imprint: Edinburgh: T. and A. CONSTABLE, Printers to His Majesty v contents [vi] blank vii–liv introduction lv chronological record [lvi] blank [1]–27 text of 'The House of Cobwebs' 28–46 text of 'A Capitalist' 47–67 text of 'Christopherson' 68–87 text of 'Humplebee' 88–105 text of 'The Scrupulous Father' 106–23 text of 'A Poor Gentleman' 124–47 text of 'Miss Rodney's Leisure' 148–74 text of 'A Charming Family' 175–91 text of 'A Daughter of the Lodge' 192–214 text of 'The Riding Whip' 215–26 text of 'Fate and the Apothecary' 227–40 text of 'Topham's Chance' [241]–64 text of 'A Lodger in Maze Pond' 265–77 text of 'The Salt of the Earth' 278–300 text of 'The Pig and Whistle,' on 300: THE END / [short rule] / Printed by T. and A. CONSTABLE, Printers to His Majesty / at the Edinburgh University Press

Binding Spine, and boards at front and back, covered in dark blue cloth. Endpapers white.

Front cover Stamped in gilt and between borders at top and bottom consisting of six horizontal lines: THE HOUSE OF COBWEBS

Spine Stamped in gilt beneath the six horizontal lines continued from front cover: THE HOUSE / OF / COBWEBS / GEORGE / GISSING / CONSTABLE / LONDON

Back cover Plain.

XXVIII

THE IMMORTAL DICKENS

THE / Immortal Dickens / BY / GEORGE GISSING / WITH PORTRAIT OF CHARLES DICKENS / [publisher's stamp] / LONDON / CECIL PALMER / 49 CHANDOS STREET, COVENT GARDEN, W.C. 2.

Collation [A]⁸B–Q⁸; 128 leaves (18.5 × 12.4); [i–x] 1–243 [244–6]

Contents [i] halftitle: THE IMMORTAL DICKENS [ii] blank [iii] titlepage [iv] imprint: FIRST / EDITION / 1925 / COPY- / RIGHT / *Printed in Great Britain* v contents [vi] publisher's statement: NOTE: Nine of the chapters in / this volume are printed / by special arrangement / with Messrs. Methuen & Co / the owners of the copyright. vii–ix introduction [x] blank 1–243 text, on 243 at foot: BRISTOL: BURLEIGH LTD. AT THE BURLEIGH PRESS 244–5 advertisements [246] blank A photograph of Dickens at the age of 23 has been pasted in between [ii] and [iii].

Binding Spine, and boards at front and back, covered in maroon cloth.

Spine On a paper label at top with and between a light floral design the words: The / Immortal / Dickens / George / Gissing / Cecil Palmer

Back and front covers Plain.

This book, dated 1924 and with an introduction and bibliography by Temple Scott, was published in North America by Greenberg, New York, under the title: *Critical Studies of the Works of Charles Dickens*.

PUBLICATION

Both *Critical Studies of the Works of Charles Dickens* and *The Immortal Dickens* are collections of the prefaces Gissing had written towards the end of his life for the Rochester edition of Dickens' work which was published by Methuen. Two months or so after returning to England, having spent the winter of 1897–8 on the Continent, he was asked to write eleven introductions of some 3000 words each and he agreed to do so, in fact writing them in three spells of work during the course of about a year and a half. Since Methuen's Rochester edition was not a success, only six of the eleven introductions were in fact used. Thus, in the two books being described here, six of the introductions were being republished and the others were being published for the first time. In the table which follows the first set of dates gives the dates of composition while the second gives the publication dates of the individual volumes in the Methuen edition.

David Copperfield	18–21 August 1898	
Dombey and Son	22–5 August 1898	
The Pickwick Papers	29–31 August 1898	December 1899
Nicholas Nickleby	22–4 September 1898	July 1900
Bleak House	February 1899	November 1900
Oliver Twist	21–3 February 1899	December 1900
The Old Curiosity Shop	16–19 June 1899	April 1901

Martin Chuzzlewit	20–3 June 1899	
Barnaby Rudge	24–6 June 1899	November 1901
Sketches by Boz	13–14 February 1900	
Christmas Books	15–19 February 1900	

Despite the efforts of B.W. Matz, editor of *The Immortal Dickens*, and of Temple Scott, editor of *Critical Studies*, two of the introductions were never found, ie, those for *David Copperfield* and *The Christmas Books*. And when the Methuen edition failed, its editor, Kitton, had asked Gissing to write a new introduction to *David Copperfield* for the Autograph Edition which was to be published in New York by G.D. Sproul [see *Related Publications* below], so that, even if the introduction to *David Copperfield* had existed, the two editors might not have been able to use it. The unpublished introductions that they could use were those for *Dombey and Son, Martin Chuzzlewit*, and *Sketches by Boz*.

The table of contents in *The Immortal Dickens* reads as folows:

Chapter	i Dickens in Memory	1–13
	ii Sketches by Boz	14–40
	iii The Pickwick Papers	41–62
	iv Oliver Twist	63–87
	v Nicholas Nickleby	88–111
	vi Martin Chuzzlewit	112–39
	vii Dombey and Son	140–63
	viii Barnaby Rudge	164–90
	ix The Old Curiosity Shop	191–218
	x Bleak House	219–43

The first chapter, 'Dickens in Memory,' was a paper collected from an earlier publication [see *Related Publications* below]. In *Critical Studies of the Works of Charles Dickens* it appears at the end of the volume.

Gissing had been offered ten guineas for each introduction and, since he was paid for all of them, he received £115.10 from which was deducted Colles' fee for handling the arrangements for some of them. Gissing's accounts show that he received £100.17.6. In New York the 1500 copies of *Critical Studies of the Works of Charles Dickens* were sold at $3 each: in England the book cost 6/-.

RELATED PUBLICATIONS

The disposition of the present bibliography is in part related to the judgement that there are only two genuine books on Dickens which were written by

Gissing. These are *Charles Dickens: A Critical Study* (XIX) and *The Immortal Dickens* (with of course its American counterpart *Critical Studies of the Works of Charles Dickens*). Now listed are Gissing's other writings on Dickens:

1 'Dickens' Homes and Haunts,' *The Nottinghamshire Guardian*, 16 August 1902. Reprinted in *Homes and Haunts of Famous Authors*, London: Darton 1906, pp 105–20. This was a commissioned essay written at the end of January 1901 for the Northern Newspaper Syndicate for a fee of six guineas.

2 FORSTER'S / LIFE OF DICKENS / *ABRIDGED AND REVISED* / BY / GEORGE GISSING / WITH PORTRAITS, ILLUSTRATIONS, AND FACSIMILES / LONDON: CHAPMAN & HALL, LD. / 1903

Gissing was unable to accept Chapman & Hall's invitation to write a life of Dickens and agreed instead to abridge Forster's for a fee of £150. Though at first he set to work with scissors and paste, he in the end corrected Forster as he went along and in some places inserted sentences and even whole paragraphs of his own. There was the minor flurry of a dispute about how much was Forster and how much Gissing, in part triggered by the fact that on both the spine and the dust cover the title was given as 'The Life of Dickens: Forster and Gissing,' but the book clearly does not represent the Life of Dickens Gissing would have written for Chapman & Hall had he wished and been free to do so. Though the book is dated 1903, it appeared on 10 October 1902. The American issue, published by McLure, Philips also appeared in 1902.

3 'Dickens in Memory,' *Literature*, 21 December 1901, pp 572–5; reprinted in *The Critic*, January 1902, pp 47–51, and later used as a chapter in both *The Immortal Dickens* and *Critical Studies of the Works of Charles Dickens*. Gissing noted this publication in his letter to Gabrielle Fleury dated 1 January 1902 (*Fleury* 146).

4 The introduction to *David Copperfield* for the Autograph Edition of Dickens' works published by G.D. Sproul in New York. Gissing mentioned his contribution to this edition in a letter to Bertz dated 15 February 1003: 'Did you see in the Athenaeum about that astounding American edition of Dickens, one set of which is to cost £20,000? I am connected with the affair, having written the Preface to *Copperfield*, and I have just *signed* 300 copies of the last sheet of the said preface. I only asked £20 for this bit of writing, and I suspect I might have got very much more' (*Bertz* 316).

5 Two reviews by Gissing are reprinted in Pierre Coustillas' *Gissing's Writings on Dickens*: 'Mr. Swinburne on Dickens,' *TLS*, 25 July 1902, p 219, and a review of Kitton's *Life of Dickens*, *TLS*, 15 August 1902, p 243. According to Coustillas, Gissing received £4 and £5 respectively for these reviews.

XXIX

SINS OF THE FATHERS

SINS OF THE / FATHERS / and other tales / By / GEORGE GISSING / [publisher's stamp] / 1924 / PASCAL COVICI, Publisher / CHICAGO

Collation [1–9]⁸10⁴ (the final leaf is used as the endpaper and is pasted to the board whereas the first leaf is not); 76 leaves (23.5 × 15.8); [i–xxic] 1–124 [125–6]

Contents [i–ii] blank [iii] halftitle: THE SINS OF THE FATHERS [iv] blank [v] titlepage [vi] copyright statement: Copyright 1924 / PASCAL COVICI: Publisher / Chicago [vii] publisher's note: *This edition is limited to 550 / numbered copies of which 500 are offered / for sale. / This copy is / No.* / [viii] blank [ix] contents [x] blank [xi–xxii] introduction [xxiii] flytitle: THE SINS OF THE FATHERS [xxiv] blank 1–31 text [32] blank 33–55 text of 'Gretchen' [56] blank 57–89 text of 'R.I.P.' [90] blank 91–124 text of 'Too Dearly Bought' [125–6] blank

Binding The spine and about 2 cms of each cover are covered in glazed straw-coloured calico. The remainder of both front and back boards is covered with heavy, mottled mauve and purple paper with a prominent black-veined effect. Endpapers plain white.

Front cover Plain.

Spine At the top of the spine is pasted on a label on which is printed in black: *The Sins of the Fathers* / GEORGE GISSING

Back cover Plain.

It is explained in the introduction that a Mr Christopher Hagerup found and identified four stories that Gissing had written for the *Chicago Tribune*. The four stories appeared on the following dates in 1877.

The Sins of the Fathers	10 March
R.I.P.	31 March
Too Dearly Bought	4 April
Gretchen	12 May

XXX

A VICTIM OF CIRCUMSTANCES

A / VICTIM OF / CIRCUMSTANCES / and other stories / BY / GEORGE GISSING / LONDON / CONSTABLE & CO. LTD / 1927

Collation [A]⁸B–U⁸; 160 leaves (18.8 × 12.4); [i]–xii [1]–308

Contents [i] halftitle: A VICTIM OF CIRCUMSTANCES [ii] publisher's advertisement [iii] titlepage [iv] imprint: *First Published 1927* / [rule] / *Printed in Great Britain by / Wyman & Sons, Ltd., London, Fakenham and Reading.* v contents [vi] blank vii–xii preface [1]–308 text

Binding Spine, and boards at front and back, covered in light blue cloth. Endpapers white.

Front cover Stamped in blue and within a small rectangle slightly above centre: A VICTIM / *of* / CIRCUMSTANCES / *by* / GEORGE GISSING

Spine Stamped in blue and within a frame which is divided at three points by horizontal rules: A VICTIM / *of* / CIRCUMSTANCES / *by* / GEORGE / GISSING / CONSTABLE

Back cover Plain.

A Victim of Circumstances, the American version of which, bound in sky blue cloth, was published by Houghton Mifflin in 1927, contains the following stories:

A Victim of Circumstances	3–36
One Way of Happiness	39–52
The Fate of Humphrey Snell	55–71
A Despot on Tour	75–98
The Elixir	91–104
The Light in the Tower	107–23
The Schoolmaster's Vision	127–44
The Honeymoon	147–64
The Pessimist of Plato Road	167–83
The Foolish Virgin	187–216
Love and Liz	219–36
The Tyrant's Apology	239–54
Spellbound	257–70
Our Learned Fellow-Townsman	273–88
Fleet-Footed Hester	291–308

XXXI

LETTERS OF GEORGE GISSING TO MEMBERS OF HIS FAMILY

LETTERS OF / GEORGE GISSING / *To Members of His Family* / COLLECTED AND ARRANGED / BY / ALGERNON AND ELLEN GISSING / WITH A

PREFACE BY HIS SON / A PORTRAIT IN PHOTOGRAVURE / AND A FACSIMILE LETTER / LONDON / CONSTABLE & COMPANY LTD. / 1927

Collation $[\pi]^4$A–Z^{8}2A–2C^8; 214 leaves (22.8 × 14.7); [i–xii] [1]–414 [415–16]

Contents [i] halftitle: LETTERS OF GEORGE GISSING [ii] half page photograph of Gissing [iii] titlepage [iv] blank v–vi preface vii publisher's note: EDITOR'S NOTE / *Portions have necessarily been omitted from / many of the letters. Except in those cases / where a definite theme has been broken into, / these omissions have not been indicated by dots.* [viii–xi] facsimile of authograph letter [xii] blank [1]–414 text [415] PRINTED IN GREAT BRITAIN BY ROBERT MACLEHOSE AND CO. LTD. / THE UNIVERSITY PRESS, GLASGOW [416] blank

Binding Spine, and boards at front and back, covered in apple green cloth.

Front cover Plain.

Spine Stamped in gilt: The Letters / of George / Gissing to / His Family / Constable

Back cover Plain.

XXXII

BROWNIE

BROWNIE / By George Gissing / Now first reprinted from The / Chicago Tribune together with / six other stories attributed to him / *With Introductions by* / GEORGE EVERETT HASTINGS / VINCENT STARRETT / THOMAS OLLIVE MABBOTT / *New* [publisher's stamp] *York* / Columbia University Press / mcmxxxi

Collation [1–9]^8[10]^7; 60 leaves, the first and last used as endpapers (24.5 × 15.7); [1–6] 7–[103] [104–110]

Contents [1] halftitle: Brownie / BY GEORGE GISSING / With six other stories attributed to him [2] blank [3] titlepage [4] copyright statement and imprint: Copyright 1931 Columbia University Press / *Published* OCTOBER, *1931* / Printed in the United States of America / By STEPHEN DAYE PRESS, Brattleboro, Vt. [5] contents [6] blank 7–[22] introduction [23]–[31] text of 'Brownie' [32]–[46] text of 'The Warden's Daughter' 47–[54] text of 'Twenty Pounds' [55]–71 text of 'Joseph Yates' Temptation' [72] blank [73]–[86] text of 'The Death Clock' 87–[93] text of 'The Serpent-Charm' 94–[103] text of 'Dead and Alive' [104] blank [105] flytitle: APPENDIX [106] blank 107 summary of contents:

Gissing's / Contributions to Chicago Newspapers [108] blank [109] publisher' statement and imprint: Brownie / FIVE HUNDRED COPIES OF THIS / BOOK DESIGNED BY VREST ORTON, SET IN / LINOTYPE BASKERVILLE, HAVE BEEN PRINTED / ON DUTCH CHARCOAL PAPER BY STEPHEN / DAYE PRESS OF BRATTLEBORO, VERMONT, / FOR THE COLUMBIA UNIVERSITY PRESS. / THIS IS COPY NUMBER / COLUMBIA UNIVERSITY PRESS / COLUMBIA UNIVERSITY / NEW YORK / [rule] / FOREIGN AGENT / OXFORD UNIVERSITY PRESS / HUMPHREY MILFORD / AMEN HOUSE, LONDON, E.C. [110] blank

Binding Spine, and about 1 cm. of front and back boards covered in brown cloth. The rest of the front and back boards covered in fawn paper spotted with green and flecked with gold. Endpapers white.

Front cover Plain.

Spine Stamped in gilt and between two simple devices: BROWNIE / George Gissing / COLUMBIA UNIVERSITY PRESS

Back cover Plain.

PUBLICATION

The introduction of this volume recounts the process by which the three editors attempted to trace Gissing's contributions to Chicago newspapers in 1877. A useful appendix, which summarized their findings, is reproduced below:

GISSING'S CONTRIBUTIONS TO CHICAGO NEWSPAPERS

This table is given to illustrate that the stories, if all are Gissing's, show a regular production and contribution during the novelist's stay in Chicago; and the delayed printing in July of two stories, one signed, left with the *Tribune* for use after his departure. (See the remarks of Mr Starrett.) It should be remembered that in gathering the stories from the files we had no expectation of discovering this orderly arrangement.

C.H. – CHRISTOPHER HAGERUP
G.E.H. – GEORGE EVERETT HASTINGS
V.S. – VINCENT STARRETT
T.O.M. – THOMAS OLLIVE MABBOTT

Table

TITLE	PAPER	DATE	REASON FOR ATTRIBUTION	COLLECTED	FINDERS
SINS OF THE FATHERS	Tribune	10 Mar.	Reprinted at Troy	Covici	C.H.; G.E.H.
R.I.P.	Tribune	31 Mar.	Style	Covici	C.H.; G.E.H.
TOO DEARLY BOUGHT	Tribune	14 Apr.	Signed	Covici	C.H.; G.E.H.
THE DEATH-CLOCK	Tribune	21 Apr.	External evidence	Here	G.E.H.
THE SERPENT-CHARM	Tribune	28 Apr.	External evidence	Here	G.E.H.
THE WARDEN'S DAUGHTER	Journal	28 Apr.	Tradition, etc.	Here	V.S.; T.O.M.
GRETCHEN	Tribune	12 May	Signed	Covici	C.H.; G.E.H.
TWENTY POUNDS	Journal	19 May	Tradition, etc.	Here	V.S.; T.O.M.
JOSEPH YATES' TEMPTATION	Post	2 June	Style, etc.	Here	T.O.M.
DEAD AND ALIVE	Tribune	14 July	External evidence	Here	G.E.H.
BROWNIE	Tribune	29 July	Signed	Here	G.E.H.

XXXIII

GEORGE GISSING AND H.G. WELLS

GEORGE GISSING / AND / H.G. WELLS / *Their Friendship / and Correspondence / Edited with an Introduction by* / Royal A. Gettmann / [publisher's stamp] / London / RUPERT HART-DAVIS / 1961

Collation [A]⁸B–S⁸; 144 leaves (20.3 × 12.8); [1–10] 11–285 [286–88]

Contents [1] halftitle: GEORGE GISSING / AND H.G. WELLS [2] blank [3] titlepage [4] copyright statement and imprint: © *The Board of Trustees / of the University of Illinois 1961 / Printed in Great Britain by Richard Clay and Company, Ltd. / Bungay, Suffolk* [5] dedication: FOR / M.H. Black [6] blank 7 contents [8] blank 9–[10] preface 11–31 introduction [32] blank 33–285 text [286–88] blank A photograph of Gissing is pasted in between [2] and [3]

Binding Spine, and boards at front and back, covered in maroon cloth. Endpapers white.

Front cover Plain.

Spine Stamped in gilt: George / Gissing / & / H.G. / Wells / Rupert / Hart-Davis

Back cover Plain.

This edition of the correspondence between Wells and Gissing from the Wells Collection at the University of Illinois at Urbana contains, in addition, correspondence between Wells and Gosse and Wells and Frederick Harrison, as well as the following appendices:

Appendix A Wells' review of *Eve's Ransom*, originally printed as 'The Depressed School,' *Saturday Review*, 27 April 1895

Appendix B Wells' review of *The Paying Guest*, which first appeared in the *Saturday Review*, 18 April 1896

Appendix C 'The Novels of Mr. George Gissing' by H.G. Wells, which first appeared in the *Contemporary Review*, August 1897

Appendix D 'George Gissing: An Impression' by H.G. Wells, the rejected preface to *Veranilda* that was first published in the *Monthly Review*, August 1904

XXXIV

THE LETTERS OF GEORGE GISSING TO EDUARD BERTZ

The Letters of George / Gissing to Eduard Bertz / 1887–1903 / edited by / ARTHUR C. YOUNG / CONSTABLE. LONDON

Collation [1]–24^8; 172 leaves (21 × 13.8); [i]–xl [1]–337 [338–40]

Contents [i] halftitle: THE LETTERS OF GEORGE GISSING / TO EDUARD BERTZ [ii] blank [iii] titlepage [iv] copyright statement and imprint: LONDON / PUBLISHED BY / *Constable and Company Ltd* / 10–12 ORANGE STREET W.C. 2 / *First Published in Great Britain* 1961 / Copyright © 1961 *Rutgers, The State University* / *Made and printed in Great Britain by* / William Clowes and Sons, Limited, London and Beccles [v] dedication: To my parents / and to Kathy [vi] blank [vii]–viii acknowledgements [ix]–xv introduction [xvi] blank [xvii]–xl textual and biographical notes [1] flytitle: The letters of George Gissing to / Eduard Bertz [2] blank 3–337 text [338–40] blank

Binding Spine, and boards at front and back, covered in black cloth. White endpapers.

Front cover Plain.

Spine Stamped in gilt: The / Letters / of / GEORGE / GISSING / to / EDUARD / BERTZ / Constable

Back cover Plain.

Professor Young notes in the introduction that the 'edition contains 189 letters and post cards written by Gissing to Eduard Bertz between April 1887 and October 1903,' a correspondence that had been purchased by Yale after a train of events described on p xv. There are two appendices: Appendix I, a letter from William Blackwood to Gissing dated 8 October 1896; Appendix II, Letters to Bertz from Gabrielle Fleury dated 24 April and 8 September 1901 and 9 October 1903.

XXXV

GEORGE GISSING'S COMMONPLACE BOOK

George Gissing's / Commonplace Book / *A Manuscript in the Berg Collection of* / *The New York Public Library* / *Edited by* / JACOB KORG / New York / The New York Public Library / 1962
Collation [1]⁴2–5⁸ (the gatherings being stapled together); 36 leaves (25.3 × 17.8); [1–6] [7]–69 [70–72]

Contents [1] halftitle: GEORGE GISSING'S COMMONPLACE BOOK [2] blank [3] titlepage [4] imprint: Library of Congress Catalog Card Number=62-12145/ Reprinted from the / *Bulletin of The New York Public Library* / September, October, November 1961 / Printed at The New York Public Library / form p 704 [i–29–63 1m] [5] contents [6] blank [7]–69 text [70] blank [71] advertisement of NYPL publications [72] blank
A photocopy of p 9 of the autograph is stapled between [2] and [3].

Binding The book has a plain, grey paper cover which has been glued to the spine.

Front cover Printed in green ink: George Gissing's / Commonplace Book

Spine Also printed in green ink: Gissing's Commonplace Book / The New York Public Library

Back cover Plain.

The nature of this publication is clearly indicated in Professor Korg's introduction. After explaining that the original from which he had made his selections is a 65-page holograph notebook in the Berg Collection of the New York Public Library, he gives a brief physical description:
'Several pages have been cut out of the front of the notebook, but the numbering of the remaining pages begins with 1. Though the entries are undated, the incidental dates which appear show that the Commonplace Book was begun

about July 1887 and continued past the publication of *Ryecroft* until the year of Gissing's death, 1903. The first fifty pages are occupied by Gissing's notes, few of them, except for extracts or summaries of reading, longer than three or four lines. There follow five unnumbered pages of short entries in the script of Gabrielle Fleury, Gissing's third wife, which are headed "Some Remarks of G.G.", and which were apprently written after his death. The pages at the back of the notebook contain miscellaneous notes . . .' (p 7). In editing the *Commonplace Book*, Korg assumed that Gissing had used it as a source-book for the writing of *The Ryecroft Papers* and therefore classified and rearranged the notebook entries so that they corresponded to the topics treated in the published book. Not all readers will agree that the *Commonplace Book* was solely a notebook used for *The Ryecroft Papers*.

XXXVI

THE LETTERS OF GEORGE GISSING TO GABRIELLE FLEURY

The Letters of George Gissing to / Gabrielle Fleury / *Edited by* / PIERRE COUSTILLAS / [device] / New York / The New York Public Library / *Astor, Lenox and Tilden Foundations* / 1964

Collation $[1-11]^8$ (the gatherings stapled together); 88 leaves (35.4 × 17.8); [1–6] 7–174 [175–6]

Contents [1] halftitle: THE LETTERS OF GEORGE GISSING TO GABRIELLE FLEURY [2] blank [3] titlepage [4] imprint: Library of Congress Catalog Card Number: 64–8185 / The Introduction and some of the / letters are reprinted from the / *Bulletin of the New York Public Library* / September, October, November 1964 / Printed at The New York Public Library / form p 724 [iii–4–65 1m] [5] contents [6] blank 7–22 introduction 23–174 text [175–6] blank

Binding The binding consists of a pink paper cover.

Front cover Diagonally across the cover and printed in gilt: The Letters / of George Gissing to / Gabrielle Fleury

Spine Printed in gilt: The Letters of George Gissing to Gabrielle Fleury

Back cover Plain.

The contents of this volume are best described by the editor's textual note which begins on p 21: 'To the best of our knowledge these letters, now

preserved in the Berg Collection, are the only ones that remain of the volu-
minous correspondence exchanged during the four periods we have previously
mentioned, but a cursory glance at the dates, whether original or supplied,
makes one immediately realize there are important gaps. Thus, it is obvious
that Gissing wrote more than two letters dated two days in succession, during
his stay in England in April 1900. Again, for the third group, correspondence
ceases on July 5 1901 though he did not leave the Sanatorium until August 10.
For the year 1898 some entries in the diary also record letters to Gabrielle
which have not been found.'

XXXVII

NOTES ON SOCIAL DEMOCRACY

NOTES ON / SOCIAL / DEMOCRACY / BY / GEORGE / GISSING /
ENITHARMON PRESS / LONDON 1968

Collation A single gathering of 16 leaves, with paper wrappers; (18.8 × 14.0);
[1–4] i–x 1–14 [15–18]

Contents [1] halftitle: ENITHARMON GISSING SERIES NO 1 [2] blank [3] titlepage
[4] copyright statement and imprint: The Enitharmon Press wishes to thank
Mr. Alfred Gissing / who has given his consent to the publication of this
volume. / Introduction © Jacob Korg 1968 / First published in 1968 by The
Enitharmon Press / 22 Huntingdon Road, East Finchley, London N.2. i–x
introduction 1–14 text [15] blank [16] publisher's note and imprint: THIS
EDITION CONSISTS OF / 400 NUMBERED COPIES / This is number   / Printed by
the Daedalus Press, / Crown House, Stoke Ferry, Norfolk. [17–18] blank

Binding A rose-pink paper wrapper.

Front cover Identical to the titlepage. The title is carried on the picture of a
banner held by a man in working clothes who stands on the shore by a pile
of tools while behind him the sun rises over a calm sea. On one of the pennant
tips of the banner are the words: WALTER CRANE. Both picture and words are
printed in black ink.

Back cover Plain.

Notes on Social Democracy, reprinted here for the first time with an introduction
by Jacob Korg, consists of three short articles which Gissing contributed to the
Pall Mall Gazette on 9, 11, and 14 September 1880.

XXXVIII

MY FIRST REHEARSAL AND MY CLERICAL RIVAL

MY FIRST REHEARSAL / and / MY CLERICAL RIVAL / by / GEORGE GISSING / [rule] / Edited and with an introduction by / PIERRE COUSTILLAS / University of Lille / LONDON / ENITHARMON PRESS 1970

Collation $1^8 2^{10}$; 18 leaves (21.2 × 14.0); [i–iv] 1–30 [31–32]

Contents [i] halftitle: MY FIRST REHEARSAL / and / MY CLERICAL RIVAL [ii] advertisement for the Enitharmon Press Gissing Series [iii] titlepage [iv] copyright statement, publisher's note and imprint: First published in 1970 / by the Enithermon Press, 22 Huntingdon Road, / East Finchley, London N.2 / Introduction © Pierre Coustillas 1970 / MY FIRST REHEARSAL was first published in *English Literature in Transition* Vol. 9 No. 1 (1966) / and acknowledgements are due to the Editor for / permission to reprint it here. MY CLERICAL / RIVAL has not been previously published. / Acknowledgements are also due to / the Berg Collection of the New York / Public Library, owners of the ms. of MY CLERICAL RIVAL. / Printed and made in Great Britain 1–11 introduction 12–20 text of 'My First Rehearsal' 21–30 text of 'My Clerical Rival' [31] publisher's note and imprint: This edition consists of 350 numbered copies. / This is No. / Printed by Stephen Austin and Sons Limited, Hertford [32] blank

Binding Spine, and boards at front and back, covered in stiff dark green morocco-patterned paper. Apple green endpapers.

Front cover Plain.

Spine Towards the top there is a small apple green label on which is printed in black: MY FIRST REHEARSAL

Back cover Plain.

XXXIX

GEORGE GISSING ESSAYS AND FICTION

George Gissing / Essays & Fiction / Edited with an Introduction by / Pierre Coustillas / *The Johns Hopkins Press* / *Baltimore and London*

Collation [1–9]^{16}; 144 leaves (22.7 × 15); [i–xiv] 1–266 [267–274]

Contents [i] halftitle: George Gissing / Essays & Fiction [ii] blank [iii] list of other books by Pierre Coustillas [iv] photograph of George Gissing [v] titlepage [vi] copyright statement and imprint: Copyright © 1970 by The Carl and Lily Pforzheimer Foundation, Inc. / 'Cain and Abel' copyright © 1970 by Alfred C. Gissing. / All rights reserved / Manufactured in the United States of America / The Johns Hopkins Press, Baltimore, Maryland 21218 / The Johns Hopkins Press Ltd., London / Library of Congress Catalog Card Number 78–100702 / International Standard Book Number 0–8018–1115–5 / This book has been brought to publication with the generous assistance of a / grant from The Carl and Lily Pforzheimer Foundation, Inc. / *The engraving reproduced on the endpapers is from* Punch *for December 8, 1887.* [vii] dedication: *To Professor Shigern Koike / of the Metropolitan University of Tokyo* [viii] blank [ix] contents [x] blank [xi] acknowledgements [xii] blank [xiii] flytitle: George Gissing / *Essays & Fiction* [xiv] blank 1–70 introduction 71–3 bibliography [74] blank 75–266 text [267–8] blank [269] publisher's note: [device] / *Designed by Arlene J. Sheer / Composed in Caslon Old Style text and display / by Typoservice Corporation / Printed on 55-lb. Perkins and Squier, Old Forge, / by the Murray Printing Company / Bound in Interlaken, ARCO Vellum / by Moore and Company, Inc.* [270–4] blank

Binding Spine, and boards at front and back, covered in green cloth flecked with silver. Endpapers green with (as stated on vi) the picture of a horsedrawn bus taken from *Punch* as the design at both front and back.

Front cover Plain.

Spine Stamped in gilt: [ornamental rule] / Doustillas / [ornamental rule] / George Gissing / [rule] / [device] / [rule]

Back cover Plain.

PUBLICATION

On p 11 of the introduction there is a statement about the sale and acquisition of the manuscripts of the nine prose works here published for the first time. The dust jacket gives more concisely than the book itself the actual contents: 'The manuscripts of the two essays in this volume – "The Hope of Pessimism" and "Along Shore" – and of five of the short stories – "All for Love," "The Last Half-Crown," "The Quarry in the Heath," "Mortimer's Choice," and "Their Pretty Way" – are owned by the Pforzheimer Library. The manuscript of "Cain and Abel" is in the Berg Collection of the New York Public Library. With one exception, "Their Pretty Way," they belong to the four years between the publication of Gissing's first and second novels.'

They are printed in the following order:

Appendixes

APPENDIX A: Summary: Gissing's Revision of His Early Work

TITLE	FIRST EDITION IN 3 VOLUMES	CONTEMPORARY PUBLICATION OF REVISED TEXT: IE, BEFORE 1903	CURRENT AVAILABILITY OF REVISED TEXT (IE, IN 1975)	AVAILABILITY OF UNREVISED TEXT (IN 1975)	PAGE REFERENCE TO DISCUSSION IN TEXT
I WORKERS IN THE DAWN	1880	Unpublished until edited by Robert Shafer for Doubleday, Doran 2 vols., 1935	Unavailable	AMS	25–9
II THE UNCLASSED	1884	Lawrence & Bullen 1895	American version by Fenno, 1895, available from AMS	Unavailable	29–32
III ISABEL CLARENDON	1886	Unpublished	Gissing's corrections of a copy of vol. I of the first edition recorded in 1969 Harvester Press edition, but not incorporated	Harvester Press 1969	32–4
V THYRZA	1887	Smith, Elder 1891	Unavailable	AMS	40–4
VII THE NETHER WORLD	1889	Minor revisions for second edition by Smith, Elder 1890	Dent 1974	Harvester Press	46–8
VIII THE EMANCIPATED	1890	Lawrence & Bullen 1893	Unavailable	AMS	49–53
IX NEW GRUB STREET	1891	English text unrevised, except for Gabrielle Fleury's translation	Unavailable	Houghton Mifflin 1962 Bodley Head 1967 Penguin 1968	53–9

Appendix B

Chronological List of Gissing's Publications to 1905

1880 *Workers in the Dawn*, 3 vols., Remington, first edition (no. I a, pp 25–6)

1884 *The Unclassed*, 3 vols., Chapman & Hall, first edition (no. II a, pp 29–30)

1886 *Isabel Clarendon*, 2 vols., Chapman & Hall, first edition (no. III a, pp 32–3)
Demos, 3 vols., Smith, Elder, first edition (no. IV a, pp 34–6). Second edition (no. IV b, p 36), in one volume in the same year

1887 *Thyrza*, 3 vols., Smith, Elder, first edition (no. V a, pp 40–1)

1888 *A Life's Morning*, 3 vols., Smith, Elder, first edition (no. VI a, pp 44–5)
Demos available from Smith, Elder in the 6/-, 3/6, 2/6, and 2/- formats (IV c, pp 36–7)

1889 *The Nether World*, 3 vols., Smith, Elder, first edition (no VII a, pp 46–7)
A Life's Morning, 1 vol., Smith, Elder, second edition (no. VI b, p 45)
The Emancipated, 3 vols., Bentley, first edition (no. VIII a, pp 49–50)
The Nether World, 1 vol., Smith, Elder, second edition (no. VII b, pp 47–8)
Reissues in the 2/6 and 2/- formats became available in the same year

1891 *New Grub Street*, 3 vols., Smith, Elder, first edition (no. IX a, pp 53–4)
Reissued in 3 volumes and called second edition (no. IX b, p 54)
New edition in one volume (no. IX c, pp 54–5). Tauchnitz same year
Thyrza, 1 vol., Smith, Elder, second edition (no. V b, p 41)
Born in Exile, 3 vols., A. & C. Black, first edition (no. XI a, pp 62–3)
Denzil Quarrier, 1 vol., Lawrence & Bullen, first edition (no. X a, pp 59–60)
Denzil Quarrier, 1 vol., Macmillan, American edition (no. X b, p 60)
A Life's Morning, 1 vol., Smith, Elder, second edition (no. VI b, p 45)

1892 *New Grub Street* and *Thyrza* available from Smith, Elder at 6/-, 3/-, 2/6, and 2/- (nos. IX d, e, f, pp 55–7)
Thyrza, 1 vol., Smith, Elder, reissue of second edition (no. V c, p 42)

1893 *The Odd Women*, 3 vols., Lawrence & Bullen, first edition (no. XII a, pp 66–7)
The Emancipated, 1 vol., Lawrence & Bullen, second edition (no. VIII b, p 50)
American version of the second edition published by Way & Williams
Born in Exile, 1 vol., A. & C. Black, reissue (p 63)

1894 *In the Year of Jubilee*, 3 vols., Lawrence & Bullen, first edition (no. XIII a, pp 70–1)
The Odd Women, 1 vol., Lawrence & Bullen, reissue (no. XXI b, p 67)
American issue by Macmillan

1895 *Eve's Ransom*, 1 vol., Lawrence & Bullen, first edition (no. XIV a, pp 73–4)
London Illustrated News, 5 Jan.–30 March. Second impression in the same year. American first edition (no. XIV b, pp 74–5), by Appleton
Sleeping Fires, 1 vol., Unwin, first edition (no. XVI a, pp 78–9). Reissued as a paperback the same year (no. XVI b, pp 79–80)
The Paying Guest, 1 vol., Cassell, first edition (no. XV a, pp 76–7) American first edition (no. XV c, pp 77–8), by Dodd, Mead
The Unclassed, 1 vol., Lawrence & Bullen, second edition (no. II b, pp 30–1). Second edition (no. II c, p 31) reissued in North America by Fenno
In the Year of Jubilee, 1 vol., Lawrence & Bullen, second edition (no. XII b, p 71)
First American edition (no. XII c, p 71), by Appleton Century is version of the second edition
The Emancipated, 1 vol., Lawrence & Bullen, third edition (no. VIII c, p 50); also Colonial Edition, 1 vol., George Bell & Sons (no. VIII d, p 51)
1896 *Sleeping Fires*, 1 vol., Appleton Century, first American edition (no. XVI c, p 80)
1897 *The Whirlpool*, 1 vol., Lawrence & Bullen, first edition (no. XVII a, p 81). Second impression . American edition by Stokes
1898 *Human Odds and Ends*, 1 vol., Lawrence & Bullen, first edition (no. XVIII a, pp 82–3)
The Town Traveller, 1 vol., Methuen, first edition (no. XX a, p 86) American edition (no. XX b, pp 86–7) by Stokes
Charles Dickens: A Critical Study, 1 vol., Blackie, first edition (no. XIX a, pp 83–4)
American first edition by Dodd, Mead
1899 *The Crown of Life*, 1 vol., Methuen, first edition (no. XXI a, pp 88–9) American edition (no. XXI b, pp 88–9) by Stokes
1901 *By the Ionian Sea*, 1 vol., Chapman & Hall, first edition (no. XXIII a, p 90) Reissue (no. XXIII b, pp 94–5), in a smaller format. Published in the *Fortnightly Review*
Our Friend the Charlatan, 1 vol., Chapman & Hall, first edition (no. XXII a, pp 91–2)
American edition by Holt (no. XXII b, pp 92–3)
Eve's Ransom, 1 vol., A.H. Bullen, reissue of old stock
New Grub Street, translated by Gabrielle Fleury, appeared as *La Rue des Meurt-de-Faim* in *Le Journal des Débats*, 23 Feb.–3 June
The Odd Women, 1 vol., A.H. Bullen, reissue of old stock
1902 *Charles Dickens: A Critical Study*, 1 vol.; this second edition was used as a volume in Gresham's Imperial Edition of the works of Dickens.

The Private Papers of Henry Ryecroft, published in the Fortnightly Review, 1 May, 1 August & 1 November 1902 and 1 February 1903

New Grub Street, translated by Gabrielle Fleury and called La Rue des Meurt-de-Faim, appeared in book form

1903 The Private Papers of Henry Ryecroft, 1 vol., Constable, first edition (no. XXIV a, pp 96–7)

First American edition by Dutton (no. XXIV b, pp 97–8)

1904 Veranilda, 1 vol., Constable, first edition

Second impression

1905 Will Warburton, 1 vol., Constable, first edition (no. XXVI, pp 102–3)

Veranilda, American issue by Dutton (no. XXV, p 101)

The Odd Women, 1 vol., A.H. Bullen, reissue of second edition (no. XII c, pp 67–8)

Index